Praise for *Joyful Defiance*

"In this book born from personal tragedy—the death of her spouse and life-changing injuries to her son—Anna Madsen offers a narrative of joy. She teaches us that in spite of death, and to spite death, joy does come to those with the courage to lament."

—Brad A. Binau, professor of pastoral theology,
Trinity Lutheran Seminary at Capital University

"What do we believe about joy? What have we been taught about grief and lament? In *Joyful Defiance*, Anna Madsen helps us to rethink emotions that may seem to chafe against faith (or at least our ideas of it). Blending Scripture, theology, and personal experience, this book reminds us that, in the words of Martin Luther's hymn 'A Mighty Fortress,' 'though life be wrenched away,' the reign of God is ours—defying death and deeply defining joy—forever."

—Elizabeth Hunter, editor, *Gather* magazine

"In a world where grief is expediently packaged, lament is shrouded by righteous vindication, and joy has become an aspiration, Madsen invites us into an opportunity to heal and to hope. In these pages, you will find your voice, your lament, your joy. Then ready yourself—for joy will defiantly lead you onward."

—Kevin L. Strickland, bishop of the Southeastern
Synod of the ELCA and former executive for worship
and assistant to the presiding bishop, ELCA

"Madsen speaks powerfully and inspirationally to lives upended by the coronavirus and current political and social upheaval, offering a master class in embodying joyful defiance amid all that threatens to undo us. Drawing from deep wells of Lutheran and liberation theologies as well as from the brutalizing grief of losing her husband and almost losing her young son in a 2004 car accident, Madsen testifies to the essential place of personal and communal lament within Christian life and practice. Learning from Madsen about not taking the beauty, grace, love, and joy for granted in our Holy Saturday existence is just the balm we need to face these uncertain days."

—DEANNA THOMPSON, director of the Lutheran
Center for Faith, Values, and Community, and
Martin E. Marty Regents Chair in Religion
and the Academy, St. Olaf College

"Anyone who has experienced thirst—dry-as-dust thirst—knows the joy of cold, refreshing water. And the joy is multiplied when one thirsty person leads another to the water. Anna Madsen's words resonate with the anguish of thirst and the joy of thirst satisfied—and offer an invitation for anyone who knows thirst: Come and read."

—DICK BRUESEHOFF,
spiritual director and retreat leader

"I love *Joyful Defiance*—the book *and* the approach to life and faith Anna Madsen presents. She explores a common hurdle for Christians about what it is to be faithful: What does it mean for my relationship with God when I am in pain and questioning my suffering? We often think of the responsibilities of our faith, none more important than to believe. Dr. Madsen shows us there is more for us there than responsibilities: there is also freedom. God with us in our suffering gives us the freedom not just to name the many deaths our suffering harbors, but also to know that pain and death do not get the last word. That honor goes to life and joy, which are indeed real-er than death."

—Char Skovland, mental health and addictions therapist
and adjunct professor, South Dakota State University

"Life is saturated with cause for lament. Let us count the ways! How do we ground our lives in joy when reasons for lament are so palpable? Anna Madsen risks joyful defiance as a way of life, not an ephemeral feeling. This book invites readers to journey toward joy in Christ Jesus, deeper than passion's agony and beyond death's silence."

—Craig L. Nessan, academic dean and William D. Streng
Professor for the Education and Renewal of the Church,
Wartburg Seminary, and author of *Free in Deed:
The Heart of Lutheran Ethics* (Fortress Press, 2022)

Joyful Defiance

JOYFUL DEFIANCE

DEATH DOES NOT WIN THE DAY

ANNA M. MADSEN

Fortress Press
Minneapolis

JOYFUL DEFIANCE
Death Does Not Win the Day

Cover image: Evan Brockett / Unsplash.com
Cover design: John Lucas Design

Print ISBN: 978-1-5064-7261-4
eBook ISBN: 978-1-5064-7262-1

To the mourners and the sufferers,
The depleted and despairing,
The exhausted and exasperated,
The dying and those who
feel already dead

———————

Were they to take our house,
Goods, honor, child or spouse,
Though life be wrenched away,
They cannot win the day.

—Martin Luther

———————

Doch. Doch. Doch.

—Karl Madsen

Contents

Introduction

When I signed the contract for this book, it was in May of 2020. The two-week Covid-19 shutdown had already extended into two months, and we were beginning to realize that "and counting" needed to be added to any new end-in-sight speculation.

Still, necessary as the shutdown was, *still*, I thought . . .

Still, I think most *everyone* thought . . .

By midfall, things should be up and running. By then we'd be back to normal. But pride goeth before the fall of 2020, because here I sit in the fall of 2021, wondering what normal *ever* was, whether there will be any semblance of it ever again and, if it brought us this pandemic and the various flavors of toxic nonsense associated with it, whether *that* normal was so particularly great after all.

As I write this introduction, over 736,000 US citizens alone and over 4.94 million worldwide have died of this highly contagious, highly preventable disease. Hundreds of thousands of businesses have closed, and small shops owned by regular people have been the hardest hit. Those run by women and people of color have been especially vulnerable to the economic effects of Covid. Despite the Paycheck Protection Program, storefronts still clinging to their keys might shutter their shops anyway, thanks to a mountain of accrued and deferred expenses or to employees whom they had to let go and who have necessarily gone on to other things.

Just as pressing of a crisis is that of the mental health ramifications of the pandemic. How many arms have ached for an embrace, eyes yearned to lay themselves on a beloved, spirits wished for the ordinary humdrum routine of the clatter of familiar people in familiar places? Conversely, how many fearful hearts have been trapped between walls filled with tension or abuse have tummies grumbled with the uncertainty of whether even a peanut butter sandwich, let alone peanut butter, can be found in the kitchen? How much cortisol has flowed through the bodies of those who should be providing for their families but cannot because they are forced to stay home to supervise distant learning or to care for children or parents and are unable to work—or work well—remotely?

Foreclosures, financial hardship, food insecurity, substance abuse, abuse of any sort, depression and other mental health issues, work-related stress, childcare stress, and not enough time alone or too much time being alone (depending on household structure)—all of these malexperiences and more have been heaped upon each of us in one way or another.

And that's just the consequences of Covid.

In the years leading up to the pandemic, as if caught in an earthquake fault, the nation found itself scathed by the friction of shifting, deeply embedded tectonic plates of racism, sexism, privilege, economic inequity, political extremism, gun violence and gun culture, ableism, heterosexism, and a culture of verbal abuse and gaslighting.

We are, individually and collectively, bruised and taut and tired and have been for some time.

Because of the work that I do as presenter and consultant across the United States and Canada, my vocational finger finds itself on the pulse of what is going on within the systems (both individually and corporately) of rostered leaders, laity, and denominations. I can't help but notice synchronous beats when they occur.

So since 2010, through my work as a public—and private—theologian, I have heard the stories of people who have questions about and for God. But since 2016, those questions have turned from being largely meta, like how to think about God, or what form the church is to be now, or how to forgive, or how to engage the "nones" (those who have no religious affiliation), to being more specific and angst filled, like how pastors who no longer want to follow their calling can keep their faith, or how to avoid letting politics end relationships (and whether sometimes ending them is unavoidable), or how to not lose hope for our country or our world. The beat these days is that we are beat. Increasingly, there's an increase in despair and a decrease in a sense of joy.

In 2004, an accident killed my late husband and gave my ever-so-young son a traumatic brain injury (TBI), and in the same awfulness, my even younger daughter thereby lost a father and the brother she had known. Ever since then, I've spent an inordinate time trying to figure out joy.

Is joy even a thing?

Was it ever, really?

After having suffered, being acutely aware of someone else's suffering, or discovering the fact that suffering can be had in a nanosecond, can one ever fully feel joy?

Ought one even experience joy again?

Can joy be held in tandem with grief?

Should we laugh when others weep?

Is pure joy a possibility or just a promise—and an empty one, at that?

The cadence of these questions became a cascade, and I became quite desperate to know, *What of joy?* But as it turned out, I learned through my children that yes, joy is a thing.

In his hymn "A Mighty Fortress Is Our God," Luther wrote of "hordes of devils" and "foes," proclaiming, "Were they to take our house, goods, honor, child, or spouse, though life be wrenched away, they cannot win the day." In theory, it sounds good and sings even better. But on June 19, 2004, spouse and child *were* wrenched away. There was nothing theoretical about my husband lying bruised and lifeless on a cold table in the bowels of a hospital or the *beep beep beep* of machines keeping my son in the land of the living. What Luther framed as fact was a question that dogged me for years: Would these hordes win the day, or would they not?

For quite some time, they threatened to do just that: wrest away the well-being of my daughter, my son, and me. The moment it finally clicked that despair could not be allowed entry into our individual and collective spirits marked the moment when I began to rethink joy.

Joy became the way to defy the devilish pieces of life, those ones that dive at you when you least expect it, those ones that at their worst can even make one want to die from the grief of it all. Joy became an antidote, a counterpoint, even—and this is something for a quasi pacifist to say—a *weapon* against despair. Joy became a defiant refusal to cede death another win by donating my essence to its cause.

The longer that my family and I practiced this way of being, the less of a conscious effort it took. We simply opted to see death, acknowledge it, grieve it, and then purposely defy it with joy. A holy neener-neener, if you will. Eventually, my small brood and I grew to understand joy as less a feeling than a way of being.

That's to say that joy is an essence that both centers and courses through someone, a posture that defines how one encounters life in all its complexities. Joy reminds a person that the present circumstances shape but do not define who one is nor how the situation at hand will ultimately pan out. Joy causes a sense of peace to wrap around distress because it concentrates the conviction that death is real but that life is real-er.

With this notion confidently in hand, even the most dastardly moments lose the potency of their final threat.

And to this latter point, I've come to realize that joy is experienced precisely when one knows something of joy's opposite. In fact, I'm of the mind that joy *can't* be experienced unless you know something of the reasons for its opposite—namely, that of lament!

Joy, you see, is not happiness.

It's not gladness.

It's not pleasure.

Joy is rather a fullness of the knowledge of what could be, what should be, and what is. It's not naive, nor is it unaware or uninterested in sorrow, grief, or anger. Instead, joy is proleptic—namely, an experience of that which is promised and therefore that which is known, albeit not in its full completeness, even now.

———

As it turns out, Christians feel guilty about lament, and we feel guilty about joy.

It's like a slipknot that tightens when one struggles. We fear that lament demonstrates a lack of trust in God's faithfulness and therefore lays bare our raw lack of faith, and we fear that joy wanders too quickly into self-indulgence, is a forced mask of plastic happiness, or at the very least selfishly disregards those who suffer while we smile. In both cases, a certain piety plays a role: on the one hand, we want to assure God and others that our faith is unquestioning, and on the other, we want to assure God and others that we are not hedonists. But neither extreme is biblical, neither extreme has theological heft, and neither extreme is healthy, spiritually or otherwise.

With all of this in mind, this book explores both lament and joy, with the hope that by its end, readers will come to find faithful expression and comfort in lament and faithful expression and community in joy.

———

Part of my role as a systematic theologian is to invite people to reflect on their belief system and see whether it holds water within itself. So if you say such-and-such a thing about God over here [waves hand broadly to the right], then you have to say it over here [waves hand broadly to the left] or rustle up a decent reason as to why you don't. As an example, then, there are evangelical Christians who are, as they refer to themselves, "pro-life." They oppose abortion because of their faith. But it turns out, looking at the rest of their social policies, these same Christians also tend to vote for people who enact policies offering less assistance to the poor and the needy and vote for the death penalty.

I have questions then, not least of all as a systematic theologian: Why do you protect an unborn baby, but the born ones less so? At what age are they unworthy, or less worthy, of protection? If we believe that all are dependent on God's forgiveness, why does a baby—still by theological definition in need of forgiveness—deserve the right to life, but a full-grown sinner not?

In contrast, while I may personally disagree with the Roman Catholic stance on abortion, I have nothing but full-on respect for the consistency of their social justice convictions: they are deeply invested in bettering social welfare systems (Nuns on the Bus, thank you very much) and are utterly and unwaveringly opposed to the death penalty (the movie *Dead Man Walking* beautifully illustrates this complexity and conviction).

In the same way, some maintain that salvation will be not for all but rather only for the righteous, or the redeemable, or the ones who have confessed Jesus Christ as their personal Lord and Savior. But if you say that Jesus is risen from the dead and promises the same for us too, then it seems that death in all forms—even unbelief, even base sinfulness, even enabling someone else's unbelief because of harm done in Christ's name—must have been conquered. That is, if there are caveats to salvation for all people no matter what, then I want to know what they are and why. To what does a tiny asterisk after "Jesus is risen! Alleluia!" refer? What is in the fine print? On what account is "Some terms and conditions may apply" applied?

Likewise, why is it that we anxiously keep making sure that we believe and do everything *just so* before we die? Why do we keep using death as the metric for postdeath salvation when the very basic and essential Christian faith claim (Jesus is risen) is that death is rendered no longer final? And moreover, when we use the term *salvation*, why do we not emphasize that the word in Greek is *soteria*, which means "health, healing, and wholeness," not "what happens after you croak"? The fundamental focus of *biblical soteria* is "what happens now." Jesus offered salvation in and through him in the moment at hand.

But salvation—health, healing, and wholeness—is *exactly* the thing one does not feel when one is in deep grief. It warrants an additional etymological note that the word *salvation* itself stems from the Latin word *salvationem*, from which we get the word *salve*, as in "balm." What are we crying out for when we grieve but salve for our spirits? What are we lamenting if not for balm for our despair? What is it for which we weep but health, healing, and wholeness?

When Christians lament, you see, we are simply crying out for salvation.

To this end, then, and to the second point, lament is not a lack of faith *but an expression of it*. It is not disrespect of God but rather *a deep trust in God*. It is leaning deeply into the bosom of God and the grace of God, a grace born out of God's abundant and boundless love for us.

Your lament, your grief, your wail, your sadness: these are immense, powerful, substantial, real. But they are not more immense, not more powerful, not more substantial, not more real than God's love for you or God's promises to you. God is in solidarity with you in your pain, experiencing the vulnerability of your despair right with you.

This last bit might jar us.

It might because the Christian tradition has been deeply shaped by a theological approach called "Christology from above"—classical theology, essentially. It asserts that God is all that is more than human—the omni-God, I call Him, and I use that male pronoun intentionally. This God is defined by traditionally masculine notions of power and authority, expressing strength through detachment and stoicism, broken only by fierce anger and constant threat. This deity is simply a Zeusian redux—hence the omni-God; omniscient, omnipresent, and omnipotent—but has become the God of much of Christianity. This god, though, is representative not of the Jewish heritage *from* which Christianity was born but of the Greek context *in* which Christianity was born. This god has everything under control and therefore has a plan for everything, and all things are going according to it. It's the god of Candide's mentor, Pangloss, who subscribed to the notion that even in the worst of circumstances, all is for the best, for we are living in the best of all possible worlds.

This sort of god is the god about which those who attempt to comfort say, usually with a slowly shaking head, "This must have been part of God's plan." And with that shake and those words, any grief one feels, any anger, any emptiness is rendered null and void, because apparently, God not just condoned but orchestrated the pain that's being endured. And also with that shake and those words, not only is comfort gone, but so is the hope of a comforting God.

To put on my systematician's hat again, if you say that God must have a plan in *one* moment, then you must be consistent that God has a plan in *every* moment . . . or come up with a decent explanation about why this moment is different. What exceptions to the divine-plan rubric might be in play for a given moment—and any others, for that matter? For example, if God is the planning type, does God have a plan when I scratch this itch or choose beef instead of chicken for my tacos? Does God have a divine plan to bring two lovers together and also for Auschwitz? Why one and not the other?

Coming at it from another angle, if God's plan is always in play, how does placing a husband and son in front of that car reconcile with Jesus who healed and Christ who was raised? How does suffering reconcile with the Creator God, who brings the delight of creatures into creation and life out of nothing and promises to bring life out of death? Laid bare here are just some of the problems with the ubiquitous idea that God plans everything and everything goes according to God's immutable plan.

But as Christians, we believe in a risen Jesus, a savior who was killed but did not stay dead, who when living dedicated his life to healing, feeding, welcoming, teaching, cajoling, and celebrating, who himself believed in a God who brought everything out of nothing and declared creation not only *tov* ("good") but *tov meod* ("very good").

Given this profile of God to which Christians subscribe, it's hard to make the case that death and despair are part of God's plan. And it's hard to make the case that God even *has* a plan. But a person *can* make a case that God has an *agenda*, a *vision* for what all things could be. And that agenda is that of life and, I do believe, of joy despite—and perhaps even to spite—death.

Just like with my last book, my editor, Scott Tunseth, deserves great kudos for his patience, tested beyond even the heartiest metrics of Christian virtues, because just like with the last book, I turned in the manuscript late. I am both embarrassed for my repeated need of his mercy and grateful for his repeated issuance of it. I am hopeful that his posture to me represents God's ways and reminds God of the same.

Elvis Ramirez, the copyeditor for this book, has a meticulous eye and a benevolent spirit. I am grateful for the ways in which his fresh and experienced eyes caught what I'd missed and saw what I hadn't seen.

It should not go without saying that any mistakes are my responsibility—some readers might notice a sparse number of adaptations of some of my previous writings, and they will also have become accustomed to noticing that mistakes and I are old friends.

Elli Cucksey, Head Librarian of the Hamma Library of Trinity Lutheran Seminary at Capital University, is not just a resource librarian, but is herself a resource. Time and again she has helped me find obscure references, quotes, and my mind. Trinity faculty, staff, and students already know of her gifts. Alums, Elli not only has gifts; she is one!

My father, who in this past year experienced serious health issues, not least of all by way of a "rare and aggressive" lymphoma, has certainly taken one for the team during this extended book-writing season. Dad has graciously suffered through a paucity of late-afternoon shared beverages, knowing I needed every spare second to keep pecking away at my keyboard. That he did so and simultaneously beat that lymphoma so that we can now make up for those missed late-afternoon shared beverages gives me tremendous joy.

While I had nose to electronic grindstone, my son, Karl, heroically slogged through distance learning—and, out of an abundance of Covid caution, sans caregivers—for the last year and a half and completely relatedly has dutifully allowed me to type beside him as he has played more Wii and more *Angry Birds* and watched more movies since March 2020 than is the recommended per-day dose for anyone, even Karl. I am thankful for his bright, forgiving, and joyful spirit and that when we play together, Chef Pig has no chance in the world. Karl graces me with abundant reasons for joy, and all the more because he shouldn't be alive to do so.

My daughter, Else, has, I do believe, made the most sacrifices of anyone, including me, to help me complete this volume. Out of solidarity with the writing of this book, she has played more Wii and more *Angry Birds* and watched more movies with Karl than even I, which is a lot, and more than the rubric of being her brother's keeper should have even in the fine print. She has also made meals, left encouraging notes, brought me random coffees as I've typed away, and most of all, lost out on some precious mama-daughter time before she left for college, all in support of my attempts to finish this book. I am so grateful that thus far, we have harnessed her incredible powers for good; otherwise, we'd all be in a mess of trouble. She is tangible joy and brings me intangible joy, and I thank God for her every day.

My beloved David has entered my world with surprise, giving me joy the likes of which I had presumed were no longer possible for me and, quite simply, until he entered my life, the likes of which I did not know *were* possible. His presence, integrity, intellect, curiosity, generosity, good humor, smile, and love both ground me and set my heart sailing. I cannot believe that I get to be on his arm.

Last, the North Shore is due my gratitude as well. It may seem odd to thank a place, but I do. I thank the woods of 808 as well as the land surrounding and the waters of Lake Superior, because they, too, ground me and set me sailing, in more ways than one. It has been said that the Lake absorbs the storms that cross the prairie. It also absorbs the storms that cross one's life. The best way I know to thank a place, though, is to en-Joy it, and that I do, every. single. day.

1

The Absence of Lamenting
the Absence of God

In 1978, the Evangelical Lutheran Church in Canada (ELCIC) and two of the predecessor bodies to the Evangelical Lutheran Church in America (ELCA)—the American Lutheran Church (ALC) and the Lutheran Church in America (LCA)—published the *Lutheran Book of Worship*, forever fondly known as either the *LBW* or the "Green Book." The Lutheran Church–Missouri Synod (LCMS) participated in the creation of it but pulled out at the very last moment, publishing its own hymnal instead.

It was a standard book of worship for well over thirty years, and in some places, it still finds a home in Lutheran pews and certainly has a place in many Lutheran homes. But here's an interesting bit of trivia about this beloved book: all the lament psalms were removed from its pages.

It's like some huge despair magnet hovered over these sacred texts and pulled up all the psalms that dealt with grief.

This unfortunate idiosyncrasy did not pass the notice of the estimable Lester Meyer, late Old Testament scholar and long-time professor of religion at Concordia College in Moorhead, Minnesota. For a spell in the 1960s, my father, George Madsen, now a retired pastor and New Testament theologian, and Les were colleagues, not just teaching students in pristine classrooms but digging through dusty soils on archaeological sites in Caesarea Maritima. That this sort of professional relationship bloomed into a friendship is something indeed: they were like the mismatched friends in *The Odd Couple*, Dad being Oscar to Les's Felix. While as far apart in personalities as Felix and Oscar, the two of them shared a fondness not just for each other but also for biblical scholarship.

Les's deep love of details and of the Psalter led him to notice the lamentable, so to speak, omission from the *LBW*, and scholar that he was, he wrote about it.[1] Even through his terribly genteel manner, honed by a Reformed heritage and academic protocol, one can still hear how profoundly miffed Les was about these editorial decisions. Straight out of the chute, Les draws attention to the section of the *LBW* entitled "The Psalms" but with the level of sarcasm that is acceptable in polite academic company.

Les pens, "The heading ['The Psalms'] is somewhat misleading, since the section does not contain *all* of the biblical psalms. . . . It would seem . . . ungrateful to complain when Lutherans who use this worship book have more than eighty percent of the Psalter so conveniently available . . . nevertheless . . ."

And with that "nevertheless," Les proceeds to (albeit politely) lambast and lament.[2]

After a deep dive into a biblical approach of study called "form criticism," Les sifts out the specific types of psalms notably absent from the book. Thirteen (46 percent, he notes, of the missing psalms) are individual psalms of lament, seven (25 percent) are community psalms of lament, and the others are psalms of judgment and variations on the lament theme. In sum, he writes, "Of the twenty-eight psalms omitted from the *Lutheran Book of Worship*, then, twenty (or 71%) are laments, while another five (or 18%) have lament-like qualities."[3]

Lutherans, or at least the Lutheran editors, it seemed, had an aversion to, were agnostic about, or were antipathetic to lament. And it led Les to wonder why. It also led him to wonder what implications would ricochet into the life of lay worshippers were they not to have access to communal lament, a question raised all the more by his incredulity that while the hymnal, the source of worship for all the people, did not have the lament psalms, the *Ministers Desk Edition*[4] did.

Relatedly, it's worth noting that neither "lament" nor "grief" is listed as a subject heading in the *LBW* hymnal index, though that oversight has been rectified in *Evangelical Lutheran Worship* (*ELW*), the most current ELCA hymnal.

To lay out his case and lay claim to his indignation, Les leads the reader on a foray into ancient Israel's sense of God. He highlights how ancient Israelites were acutely aware of both God's presence and God's hiddenness. The latter moments, those occasions when God seems absent or is even the author of individual and communal suffering, are the ones that gave birth to the lament psalms. Who among us hasn't asked where God is in the midst of grief, tragedy, and profound suffering? Were broken hearts, lowered heads, and raised fists experiences known only to ancient Israelites? Of course not.

Like the ancient Israelites, we are more than familiar with grasping and gasping for sense, for yearning that order be regained, for praying that God be revealed and present again. Instead of shalom, we know all too well and all too often evil, suffering, inequity, death, and general but persisting nonsense. Meyer believed that for Israel—and, arguably, for us—if "all responsibility must finally rest with the one God who, as Creator, was guarantor of an orderly world . . . an orderly world testified to the divine presence."[5]

The lack of this purported orderly world, though? These moments where nothing but an echo is heard *precisely* when the Divine ought to be speaking? The apparent chaos and void shake our understanding of ourselves, of what in life can be trusted, and of whether, in fact, even God can be trusted.

Les fully understood the disillusionment that suffering can cause and knew that the ancient Israelites did as well. For them, Les writes, when this evil, suffering, death, inequity, despair, and nonsense came to pass, these moments of despair "raised the problem of the integrity of [Israel's] religious outlook."[6]

Every time I read that sentence, I am struck by Les's choice of the word *integrity*. It's a powerful word and intentionally used. If someone has no integrity, they are capricious and dishonest and cannot be trusted. To question the integrity of their faith and thereby the integrity of God, then, is no small thing. However, it is precisely what lament gives us the freedom, language, and cadence to do. Is our God worthy of the worship and faith God invites and even commands of us, or is God instead base, fickle, deceitful, cruel, and not to be trusted?

The audacity of posing such questions—directly to God, no less—is quite foreign to Christianity, as is questioning God at all. I think we are afraid of this kind of raw expression of pain and anger because we—even we Lutherans who ostensibly are all about grace—even we, at the end of the day, are not entirely sure that God can or will absorb or even tolerate our lament and what underlies it. Part of us wonders, What if we doubt, what if we end up disbelieving, and what if we then in that moment die? Then what will God do to us? Or what if our dismay is perceived by God as audacious, and what if we cause God offense, even we who believe? What will God have of us when we are met by the Divine?

Or to circle back to the introduction, what if it's true that God has an immutable plan, and all things, even horrible, painful suffering, are going according to it? What if our pain is *supposed* to happen, if we *deserve* the suffering, if we are to *learn* something from the trauma?

Lament can feel dangerously unfaithful, disobedient, or lacking in trust, and given that at least two and maybe three generations of Lutherans grew up without ready access to lament as a facet of faith (at least in the hymnal), it certainly feels foreign.

But it's not foreign to the Jewish tradition. In fact, not only did ancient Hebrews write the book—quite literally—on lamentations, but the act of lamenting is, as Les Meyer knew, a foundational part of the book of Psalms because they experienced reasons for lament in their daily lives. For this reason, Les made sure to mention in his article the late Old Testament scholar Robert Davidson, who wrote—notably in a book called *The Courage to Doubt: Exploring an Old Testament Theme*—that the experience of God's assumed absence reveals that the ancient people collectively knew of the excruciating sense that God had abandoned them and had given them up to their sins and their sufferings. With that shared lived experience, Davidson viewed the questions "Why?" and "How long?" "to be as authentic cries as 'Hallelujah.'"[7]

Christians are familiar with alleluia, of course. We get alleluia. We are all over alleluia. It may not be coincidental that the rise of contemporary Christian praise music in Lutheran circles overlapped the use of the *LBW*'s codified rejection of lament.

But Old Testament scholar Walter Brueggemann is annoyed to no end that Christians easily run to the *praises of God* but away from the *laments to God*. Dipping into the anguish of Psalm 22:1, Jesus, the Jew, himself cried out, "My God, my God, why have you forsaken me?" It passes the attention of neither Meyer nor Brueggemann that those who suffer and who claim Jesus as Savior are far less inclined than their Jewish siblings to join in that same cry to that same God.

Meyer uses Brueggemann to make his case about the absence of the lament psalms in the *LBW*. He draws upon Brueggemann's chastisements of Christians for their unwillingness to engage lament. With almost the same level of proper academic constraint as coursed through Meyer, Brueggemann laments that much Christian piety and spirituality is romantic and unreal in its positiveness. . . . It is no wonder that the church has intuitively avoided these psalms. They lead us into dangerous acknowledgment of how life really is. They lead us into the presence of God where everything is not polite and civil. They cause us to think unthinkable thoughts and utter unutterable words. Perhaps worst, they lead us away from the comfortable religious claims of "modernity" in which everything is managed and controlled. In our modern experience, but probably also in every successful and affluent culture, it is believed that enough power and knowledge can tame the terror and eliminate the darkness.[8]

It is possible, he prods us to think, that the lament psalms force us to recognize, and then articulate, our most repressed instincts, unacknowledged emotions, basest elements, and greatest fears of who we are and of the nature of the human condition. In so doing, of course, we are honest with ourselves and with God, stripped of pretensions and politeness, and raw with pain and fury.

But the Hebrew people, says Brueggemann, knew and were quite comfortable with the concept that they could honestly speak neither of life nor of God if the unpleasant parts of each weren't also uttered: their deep suffering and grief, their anger at losses and betrayals of trust, and compounding it all, a palpable absence of God's presence and redemption in its midst.

Precisely through Israel's lamentations, Brueggemann believes that by their stark candor, their verbal recollection of a life without misery, and their willingness to hold God accountable to their expectations of God, Israel "bears witness" before God. Lamenting, then, is an *act* of faith rather than a *betrayal* of it. "In that act," Brueggemann says, "God is summoned relentlessly into the now."[9]

This *nowness* is key to lament and key to the difference between Jewish and Christian embracing of it. For a series of interwoven and complicated reasons, Christians have tended to focus faith in God's redemptive action upon what happens *after death*. Our trust in redemption has become primarily futuristic in nature and in hope, the purpose of Christian baptism and belief becoming centered on a salvation that will occur after a person of faith has taken their last breath.[10]

But salvation understood primarily as something to be experienced after death was neither Jesus's faith nor his teaching—nor was it that of the Jewish religious tradition from which he came. Rather, salvation from God enters reality to meet the unwelcome presence of disease, suffering, and brokenness. Where the latter was experienced, God was committed to usher in the former, and lamentations were there to remind God precisely of those truths. Psalm 77 is a prime expression of trust that God will absorb people's pain:

> I cry aloud to God,
> > aloud to God, that he may hear me.
> In the day of my trouble I seek the Lord;
> > in the night my hand is stretched out without wearying;
> > my soul refuses to be comforted.
> I think of God, and I moan;
> > I meditate, and my spirit faints. Selah
> You keep my eyelids from closing;
> > I am so troubled that I cannot speak.
> I consider the days of old,
> > and remember the years of long ago.
> I commune with my heart in the night;
> > I meditate and search my spirit:
> "Will the Lord spurn forever,
> > and never again be favorable?

Has his steadfast love ceased forever?
　　Are his promises at an end for all time?
Has God forgotten to be gracious?
　　Has he in anger shut up his compassion?" Selah
And I say, "It is my grief
　　that the right hand of the Most High has changed."
I will call to mind the deeds of the Lord;
　　I will remember your wonders of old.
I will meditate on all your work,
　　and muse on your mighty deeds.
Your way, O God, is holy.
　　What god is so great as our God?
You are the God who works wonders;
　　you have displayed your might among the peoples.
With your strong arm you redeemed your people,
　　the descendants of Jacob and Joseph. Selah
When the waters saw you, O God,
　　when the waters saw you, they were afraid;
　　the very deep trembled.
The clouds poured out water;
　　the skies thundered;
　　your arrows flashed on every side.
The crash of your thunder was in the whirlwind;
　　your lightnings lit up the world;
　　the earth trembled and shook.
Your way was through the sea,
　　your path, through the mighty waters;
　　yet your footprints were unseen.
You led your people like a flock
　　by the hand of Moses and Aaron.

In this psalm and in so many other psalms of lament, we see that the petitioner, without varnish, asks whether God can be trusted and, relatedly, whether faith in this God is well placed. For example, "Has his steadfast love ceased forever? Are his promises at an end for all time?" (Ps 77:8) and "Has God forgotten to be gracious? Has he in anger shut up his compassion?" (Ps 77:9). The rapid-fire cadence of the questions only amplifies their desperate intensity.

But that the psalmist even *questioned* God might cause a sharp intake of breath.

The late philosopher Dr. Thomas Christenson, friend and colleague of both Les and my father as a professor at Concordia during these same years, preached there a chapel sermon on this psalm, in which he said, "It is unfortunate that we do not have a place in our liturgy for the asking of questions. We *confess* our sin, *proclaim* God's grace, *preach* God's word, we praise, witness, affirm, and so on. But we have no sacred occasion for questions, no rite of puzzlement. Yet there are all sorts of biblical models for asking serious questions."[11]

No rite of puzzlement.

Despite these biblical models and a theological heritage of questions raised in lament—laments of grief and sadness, of loss and fear—questions have not, for Christians, become liturgical.

In fact, there are few, if any, places in Christian worship where he sees where doubt, dismay, disbelief, or disillusionment are regularly identified, lifted up, given room to be aired, or even allowed to hang in the air more than by way of a passing recitation. On these occasions, preached Christenson, like the rhetorical questions posed at baptisms, the moment is "itself quite empty for lack of the real possibility of saying 'No!'" These perfunctory answers, he says, simply display the ritualistic "sacrifice of our basic human honesty and openness to others to the pretense of piety." He continues, "[But] would it not be good for a congregation to hear its pastor (on occasion) say, 'I can't make head nor tail of the Gospel text, so I'll talk about the epistle text'?

We all know that pastors sometimes think this, but no one ever says it. Would it not be good for a class to hear a teacher say, 'I can't understand this lesson, can anyone else make sense of it'? We labor under the weight of much self-assigned infallibility."[12]

It's risky to admit that *God* might be fallible. It's risky to admit that *we are* fallible. But it's safe to avoid the questions altogether. Lament psalms don't care about any of that. In lament psalms, questions are posed, uncertainty is splayed out for all to see, answers from God are impatiently awaited, irritation and even anger at God are palpable.

The thing of it is, although we are removed from the lives and ways of these ancient people in time and place, we are not in terms of experience: we too know of unwelcome and unexpected death; we too know disease that ravages the bodies of those whom we love and even our own; we too know of unjust powers that wield malevolent power; we too know of the angst of sin that we suffer as both victims and oppressors; we too know the losses of relationships, dreams, and treasured realities; we too know of unabated fury at those who have harmed us or others.

So it is curious, given our shared experience with our Jewish forebears in faith, that we excise from our communal worship the acknowledgment of—let alone the practice of—lament.

The key mark of faith seems to be not to worry and instead be happy.

The Visceral and Kinetic Energy of Lament

In the age of selfies, one does not tend to post pictures of lamenting. Who would want to make public red eyes, tear-stained cheeks, snot spilling from one's nose, or breath that can't be caught?

But that is the picture of grief. Snapshots of rage are not much better. Narrowed eyes, hollered words, uncontrolled sobs, raised fists, rocking bodies.

Joy shows different realities, ones far more palatable and postable: smiles, whoops of delight, hugs, raised hands in celebration, rocking bodies in dancing. In the picture of despair, our bodies reveal what we've lost: love, a loved one, security, trust, home. In joy, they reveal what we've found: love, reunion, community, safety, home. In both, our bodies reveal our deepest emotions and therefore our deepest selves.

The way our bodies respond in joy, you see, is far more acceptable to express in public than the way they reveal grief. Even the simple, human, common experience of crying moves people to apologize: "I'm so sorry," we say, embarrassed when the tears can't be kept brimmed behind the barriers of our eyes.

Cornel West, though, says that the Black experience of grief and loss and suffering—quite literally em-bodied in Black music, Black preaching, and Black rhetoric—makes lament not just acceptable but accessible. Of the spirituals, he writes,

> The lyrical focus is often the liberating power of God, but the stylistic forms stress the self-invested moan, the risky falsetto and the nuanced syncopation . . . the spirituals directly confront existential dread and despair with the armor of vocal virtuosity, rhythmic facility and faith in God. Subsequent developments such as the blues, jazz and gospel music may reject or revise the Christian commitment, vocalize instruments and add more complex rhythms, but the cultural crucible of such developments rests in the distinct articulation of Afro-American Christianity. . . . Black preaching of the gospel is rhythmic, cathartic and full of moans and groans. Black rhythm is rooted in religiosity, liminality and full of call and response. And the

gospel is understood in terms of existential self-involvement, moral flexibility and political improvisation.[13]

These primary expressions of the Black experience regularly and intentionally manifest loss related to the separation of Self and "home" because of African Americans' history with this exact separation. To be so familiar with loss is to speak it, to cry it, to dance it, to sing it, to groan it, all having become as natural as breathing itself. In this way, lament is embodied grief and a wailed yearning for home.

———

Over five hundred years ago, in his Heidelberg Disputation, Martin Luther wrote:

19. That person does not deserve to be called a theologian who looks upon the invisible things of God as though they were clearly perceptible in those things which have actually happened [Rom. 1–20].
20. He deserves to be called a theologian, however, who comprehends the visible and manifest things of God seen through suffering and the cross.
21. A theologian of glory calls evil good and good evil. A theologian of the cross calls the thing what it actually is.[14]

The context here was his defense of his Ninety-Five Theses and his conviction that we cannot earn our salvation, nor can we trust things valued by the world as evidence of God. It is far too easy for us to confuse our understandings and expectations of the good and our understandings and expectations of God with God. Instead, Luther said, the cross reveals that we can only be certain that God is present in the midst of suffering.

Dr. West and Dr. Luther are of one accord here. Dr. West says the spirituals, along with the blues and jazz, call a thing what it is. Their rhythms and keys and cadences give permission and pay homage to those who have endured and are enduring, and they sing God into a circumstance of grief.

It is nothing short of a scriptural tradition, this calling a thing what it is. Lamentations 1:2 drips with Jerusalem's manifest, vulnerable grief:

> *She weeps bitterly in the night,*
> *   with tears on her cheeks;*
> *among all her lovers*
> *   she has no one to comfort her;*
> *all her friends have dealt treacherously with her,*
> *   they have become her enemies.*

Job curses the day he was born, as in Job 3:1–16:

Job opened his mouth and cursed the day of his birth. Job said:

> *"Let the day perish in which I was born,*
> *   and the night that said,*
> *   'A man-child is conceived.'*
> *Let that day be darkness!*
> *   May God above not seek it,*
> *   or light shine on it.*
> *Let gloom and deep darkness claim it.*
> *   Let clouds settle upon it;*
> *   let the blackness of the day terrify it.*
> *That night—let thick darkness seize it!*
> *   let it not rejoice among the days of the year;*
> *   let it not come into the number of the months.*
> *Yes, let that night be barren;*
> *   let no joyful cry be heard in it.*
> *Let those curse it who curse the Sea,*

> *those who are skilled to rouse up Leviathan.*
> *Let the stars of its dawn be dark;*
> > *let it hope for light, but have none;*
> > *may it not see the eyelids of the morning—*
> *because it did not shut the doors of my mother's womb,*
> > *and hide trouble from my eyes.*

> *"Why did I not die at birth,*
> > *come forth from the womb and expire?*
> *Why were there knees to receive me,*
> > *or breasts for me to suck?*
> *Now I would be lying down and quiet;*
> > *I would be asleep; then I would be at rest*
> *with kings and counselors of the earth*
> > *who rebuild ruins for themselves,*
> *or with princes who have gold,*
> > *who fill their houses with silver.*
> *Or why was I not buried like a stillborn child,*
> > *like an infant that never sees the light?"*

And in a passage not often read in Christian worship, Psalm 137 boldly goes where Christians rarely have gone before, even admitting a desire for ruthless vengeance on infants:

> *By the rivers of Babylon—*
> > *there we sat down and there we wept*
> > *when we remembered Zion.*
> *On the willows there*
> > *we hung up our harps.*
> *For there our captors*
> > *asked us for songs,*
> *and our tormentors asked for mirth, saying,*
> > *"Sing us one of the songs of Zion!"*

How could we sing the Lord's song
  in a foreign land?
If I forget you, O Jerusalem,
  let my right hand wither!
Let my tongue cling to the roof of my mouth,
  if I do not remember you,
if I do not set Jerusalem
  above my highest joy.

Remember, O Lord, against the Edomites
  the day of Jerusalem's fall,
how they said, "Tear it down! Tear it down!
  Down to its foundations!"
O daughter Babylon, you devastator!
  Happy shall they be who pay you back
  what you have done to us!
Happy shall they be who take your little ones
  and dash them against the rock!

Wishing that babies would be dashed upon a rock? One could call that many things, but is that really calling it like it is? Many other adjectives could—and arguably should—instead be used to describe that sentiment, like perverse, cruel, or despicable.

And yet here's Psalm 79, with the same whiff of vengeance:

O God, the nations have come into your inheritance;
  they have defiled your holy temple;
  they have laid Jerusalem in ruins.
They have given the bodies of your servants
  to the birds of the air for food,
  the flesh of your faithful to the wild animals of the earth.
They have poured out their blood like water
  all around Jerusalem,

and there was no one to bury them.
We have become a taunt to our neighbors,
mocked and derided by those around us.

How long, O Lord? Will you be angry forever?
Will your jealous wrath burn like fire?
Pour out your anger on the nations
that do not know you,
and on the kingdoms
that do not call on your name.
For they have devoured Jacob
and laid waste his habitation.

Do not remember against us the iniquities of our ancestors;
let your compassion come speedily to meet us,
for we are brought very low.
Help us, O God of our salvation,
for the glory of your name;
deliver us, and forgive our sins,
for your name's sake.
Why should the nations say,
"Where is their God?"
Let the avenging of the outpoured blood of your servants
be known among the nations before our eyes.
Let the groans of the prisoners come before you;
according to your great power preserve those doomed
to die.
Return sevenfold into the bosom of our neighbors
the taunts with which they taunted you, O Lord!
Then we your people, the flock of your pasture,
will give thanks to you forever;
from generation to generation we will recount your
praise.

But the uncomfortable truth is, if we are honest with ourselves, we too have said terrible things, like "Damn you," or "I could kill her," or "I wish he were dead," or "I wish I were dead." Rarely do we actually mean such awful words. In the moment, though, this admitted ugliness reveals our deepest, most terrible hurt. On more than one occasion in his own writing, Brueggemann points to such passages as honest expressions of human experience, raw and unfiltered and unvarnished, just like those aforementioned lamenting selfies that none of us post. "The utterance," he writes, "is not merely catharsis, though it is that. It is also a practice of prayer that is honest and courageous. These speech practices offer an opportunity for brutalizing loss to be turned into an act of faith that may in turn issue into positive energy. These speech practices provide a way to do something with our brutalizing rage at loss so that it does not escalate into anti-neighborly hurt."[15]

Brueggemann's point here is that the power of lament provides us an outlet to express our despair and rage by directing our misanthropic emotions to God instead of to the objects of our wrath, even if these objects are ourselves. These verses call a thing what it is in the hopes that we will not instead call something quite horrible into being.

The expression of anger as lament is even more taboo than the expression of grief. It is not a polite emotion, particularly in a culture of niceness. Writing as a Minnesotan, I am here to attest that anger is not Minnesota nice. Nor is it tactful. Nor is it "appropriate."

Christians—people who tend to be far more comfortable with the sweet and genteel depiction of a smiling Jesus with a sheep around his neck than with an enraged Jesus calling his opponents a brood of vipers—are prone to believe that we, too, should just be nice. Yet the truth is that we are all, in many and various ways, steeped in anger, like a bag of tea left too long in the cup, the hot beverage becoming thick and bitter. But we tend to drink that tea anyway, lips pursed in both disgust and forced politeness.

"No, no, it tastes fine, really," we say, swallowing the sludge down with a taut smile. "Everything is fine. Everything is awesome," we say politely. Of course, everything is anything but fine, and few things are awesome.

Our ambivalence about anger has to do with many things, I believe. Anger is not polite; it causes conflict and forces people to wrestle in the open with disagreement—to own what one says and to dispute that which is claimed by another. And so it is better, we tend to think, to gloss the problem over.

To ignore it.

To pretend it doesn't exist.

The trouble is, reasons for anger do exist. There are legitimate reasons—not least of all during these deeply troubled, troubling days—to be angry and, like Jeremiah, like the psalmist, to be angry precisely in the very name of God.

Recently, I picked up Soraya Chemaly's book *Rage Becomes Her*.[16] Chemaly has dived into the study of women's anger: the way women suppress it, the way it is disdained and disallowed by the world, and how instead, women and the world ought to rather pay acute attention to it.

In 2013, when George Zimmerman was acquitted of the 2012 murder of Trayvon Martin, Alicia Garza inadvertently founded the Black Lives Matter movement, simply by ending a Facebook post rueing the verdict with the words "Black lives matter." Seven years later, the hashtag #BLM adorns T-shirts and pins and bumper stickers, and people are walking the streets, kneeling in stadiums, and postponing games—and it's painfully clear that we still need to do all of these actions and more.

Chemaly spoke with Garza about her activism and about what inspires her to engage with the powers that be. Garza replied, "Anger at injustice is one part of what motivates me. But it is not a sustainable emotion in and of itself. It has to be transformed into a deep love for the possibility of who we can be. Anger can be a catalyst, but we cannot function on anger alone. When it's not used properly, it can quickly become destructive. That's why love is important: love connects us to what we most care about; what we yearn for."[17] It's a sentiment that echoes Brueggemann above: lament is a holy vent so that the unholy does not take place.

Garza and Chemaly agree that anger lets a person know that something is off: there is an unacceptable distance—homesickness?—between what is and what should be. Justice is wanting, and righteousness is therefore too. And anger is an indication that you care enough to notice, to react, and to do something about the disconnect at hand.

Chemaly writes, "Anger has a bad rap, but it is actually one of the most hopeful and forward thinking of all our emotions. It begets transformation, manifesting our passion *and* keeping us invested in the world. It is a rational *and* emotional response to trespass, violation, and moral disorder. It bridges the divide between what 'is' and what 'ought' to be, between a difficult past and an improved possibility. Anger warns us viscerally of violation, threat, and insult."[18]

Her book begins with the story of a young Chemaly discovering her mother throwing her wedding china off a hill in their backyard. Chemaly returned to the house—and later so did her mother—with not a trace of disarray about her. About this incident, Chemaly writes, "[My mother] was getting her anger 'out,' but in a way that explicitly separated it from her relationships. Most women report feeling the angriest in private and interpersonal settings. They also prioritize their relationships—at home, work, and even in political contexts—in determining, consciously or not, if and how to express negative emotions."[19]

In a tradition that is generally conflict averse, if we acknowledge our anger at all, we have learned to toss our respective metaphorical plates in privacy. But research shows that the release of anger—not least of all by cursing—raises one's ability to tolerate pain. Perhaps that is what the ancient psalmists were doing when they sang such abhorrent wishes of vengeance. Perhaps they knew what modern scientists know: venting releases steam that would otherwise blow someone, or something, up.

Perhaps lamenting is like holy swearing. Brueggemann believes that lament might serve precisely that purpose, and looking at the culture of today, he sees the danger of misdirected anger, fury unleashed not at God but rather at one another. Much of lament is rooted in loss, and he believes that collective loss—even loss that should happen and should have happened long ago—causes outbreaks of toxic rage. These days, the loss of white male privilege manifests itself in "family abuse, in absurd armament programs and budgets, in abusive prison policies, in passion for capital punishment, and in assaults upon the poor in the name of 'reform.' All of these, I submit, are displaced practices of anger that predictably end in brutality."[20]

So what would properly placed practices of anger look like? Instead, it ought to, says Brueggemann, be directed to God and do as the ancient Israelites did, who knew to "dare to say out loud how overwhelming is the loss, how great the anxiety, how deep the consequent fear."[21] That's a liturgical move and a communal need.

Perhaps it is time to learn to lament, to console, and to hope together in regular, communal worship, not just on Good Friday, not just at funerals, but as a regular habit of gathering as the Communion of the Saints.

Liturgy and Lament

Liturgical theologian Rev. Dr. Gordon Lathrop believes that Christian worship tends to involve eight different elements:

(1) words and communally recognizable symbols, each of which in its unique way manifests the grace of God, ought to be present; (2) it ought to be held on Sunday, the day of the week that marks the New Creation brought about by the resurrection; (3) it should represent and welcome all people of God; (4) it should be grounded in tradition rather than springing up with rootless, faddish practices; (5) it should be simple; (6) it should involve ritual and internal rhythm; (7) it should proclaim the risen Christ; and (8) it should demonstrate that the Christian faith reflects and is relevant for life.[22]

While books could be written on each of these liturgical claims, it is the eighth point that interests me in the moment. Liturgy literally means the work of the people (*li-* from *laos*, a Greek word for "people," and -*urgy* from *ergos*, Greek for "work"). Liturgy is the communal practice of the people of God bringing forth their worship of God and being sent out to be refreshed servants of God.

Our standard worship involves several basic elements to its structure: the Invocation, the Confession, the Kyrie, the Lessons, the Sermon, the Creed, the Prayers, the Sharing of the Peace, the Offering, the Eucharist, and the Blessing.

Each facet of the liturgical rhythm has its key and holy role: establishing this moment in time as one in which God is expressly present, a cleaning of our consciences and an admission of our dependence on God's grace, a song of praise that lifts up our gratitude, readings that steep us in the story, a sermon that speaks the story to us in a new way, a reminder of our fundamental statements of faith, prayers for the people of God, an expression of the reign of God, a return of thanks to share with the creation of God, a celebratory meal hosted by God, and a benediction to send us out for another week as servants of God.

But it is striking how there is no ritualistic place for the expression of the complexities of *life*—namely, the laments and the joys we encounter and bring to church every week. The weekly Prayers of the People name events and people, to be sure, but rarely from our own voices; we find our griefs expressed at funerals or, conversely, at weddings or baptisms. In a customary liturgy, there is very little precedent or positivity for the opportunity to reflect on what we've lost, let alone what we've found, week to week, from either a personal or a communal experience.

Barbara Ehrenreich's book *Bright-Sided: How the Relentless Promotion of Positive Thinking Has Undermined America* was born into being because Ehrenreich suffered breast cancer. While the entire experience for her was horrific, she was most particularly appalled at the expectation that she feel buoyant, positive, and thankful for the toughness earned and the lessons learned through her disease.

She didn't particularly want to feel any of those.

She wanted to lament, to complain, to be angry: "Breast cancer, I can now report, did not make me prettier or stronger, more feminine or spiritual. What it gave me, if you want to call this a 'gift,' was a very personal, agonizing encounter with an ideological force in American culture that I had not been aware of before—one that encourages us to deny reality, submit cheerfully to misfortune, and blame only ourselves for our fate."[23]

Her book brought me back to a conversation I had with a dear woman in my world who, in her 80s, had suffered a stroke. That event took away much of her remarkable ability to create art, to amble around finding quirky gifts for even quirkier relatives and friends, to write, and to read letters sent to her by her many grandchildren. Something of her brightness of being left her when she suffered that stroke.

Naturally, people were worried. Trouble was, they had the audacity to express it, even asking whether she might be depressed. One day, when I visited her, she said, "Anna, I am so tired of people asking me if I'm depressed! Finally, I had to holler at them, 'Of course I'm not depressed! I'm a Christian!'"

To which I responded with my typical flair for pastoral care (which is to say, I am not good at it at all), "What the hell."

But I don't think that this woman is alone in her aversion to naming her pain (even to herself). Christians are so awfully wrapped up in making a person feel better or making ourselves feel better that we don't allow for the sacred space of lament. Where better to lift up our communal experience of lament than in communal worship? Sometimes I do believe that we might be so ready to leap to Easter that we ignore that we are leaping over a grave.

Were Christians to be more overt and more intentional about recognizing faults, regret, sadnesses, anxiety, fears, and the possibility that healing might not come—and what's up with that?—perhaps trust could be built up so that maybe, just maybe, this group can understand and allow for pain.

Ehrenreich's experience indicted me too. After the accident, I wrote extensive updates about Karl's healing. At the end of almost every entry, I would write, "God is good"—that is, until someone who had himself also suffered too much asked me, "How do you know? On what basis are you judging that? I prefer to simply say that God is God."

It was an interesting comment because then I was invited to express my deeply grieved and astonished and angry Self to God honestly. And what I wanted to say to God was exactly what I said to this woman close to my heart: What the hell?

If a relationship is as it claims to be, then my figuring suggests that there has to be some relating. There are reasons for people to be upset with God, because, as the ancient Israelites knew, God's promises aren't apparently living up to God's reality. I can't help but wonder if some authenticity is surrendered when there is no room for sacred lament. That said, I do realize that not everybody needs to wrestle with God. Some are quite content and quite faithful in their pure and unquestioned faith. For the rest of us, however, I'm thinking that if one can say to God, "I am really hurting here, and I feel betrayed by you, and 'soon' and 'very soon' clearly is not soon enough," then there's the beginning of renewed trust.

Annie Dillard gets to the matter in *Holy the Firm* when she retells the following story: "Once, in the middle of the long pastoral prayer of intercession for the whole world—for the gift of wisdom to its leaders, for hope and mercy to the grieving and pained, succor to the oppressed, and God's grace to all—in the middle of this [the pastor] stopped, and burst out, 'Lord, we bring you these same petitions every week.' After a shocked pause, he continued reading the prayer. Because of this, I like him very much."[24] In that moment, the pastor not only expressed his own authenticity but allowed others to be authentic too. I read that, and I think, *There's* honesty. *There's* a man I can trust. *There's* a man who probably wanted to but couldn't say in the Prayers of the People (of all things), "What the hell?"

Particularly after the dreadful last years of upheaving political and pandemic life, staring at an uncertain future still affected by this horrible virus—so much lost, so much taken away, so much missed—what would it look like to have a ritual lament in our liturgy? To set aside intentional communal time to ask God and one another, "What the hell?"

Where would it be placed? Before the Confession would suggest that lament is something that is unacceptable to feel. That is not ideal. I wonder whether we could instead form a ritual, communal lament around our Prayers of the People, or perhaps connected to our offerings, or maybe even as part of the extension of peace.

Brueggemann, treasuring the legacy—and arguably the litany—of the ancient Israelites, has wondered about the ways in which the church can serve as a place where lament is as welcome as the people in the pews are. Precisely in the context of homelessness, Brueggemann asserts that the church,

- when it is attentive to its memory;
- when it remembers its ancient miracles that it continues to treasure;
- when it has the courage to speak its own cadences rather than the accents of everyone else's language;
- when it reengages old seasons of hurt that are still poignant in our awareness;
- when it recalls its deep insistences against the Holy One;

that is, when the church accepts its own past life with God, it has ways of speaking and ways of knowing and ways of imagining that could matter in the present cultural dislocation. I propose that the church has available precisely the rhetorical and testimonial antidotes to the current emergency of *denial* and *despair*.[25]

That phrase, "that could matter in the present cultural dislocation," catches my breath every time. I often say that theology doesn't matter unless it matters. Brueggemann is saying that theology matters and, moreover, that the church actually has within its reach such antidotes. Communal worship, liturgy, is one means to administer it to that which gives rise to lament.

But as it stands, we tend to restrict the liturgical expression of lament to funerals, Lent, and Good Friday. On Ash Wednesday, even, we mark our mortality on our foreheads.

Of course, if we are honest, death is not just a yawning abyss in the future: rather, it laces itself throughout every day. And Good Friday isn't just a once-a-year deal: it can range from a crisis lasting from a relatively small sliver of time to a twenty-four-hours-a-day /

seven-days-a-week / fifty-two-weeks-out-of-every-interminable-year deal.

How can we honor these as legitimate Lenten and life experiences? What if we gave Lent room for the lament of those who cry out for mercy not because of guilt but because of grief, of brokenheartedness, of broken relationships, of loneliness, of exhaustion, of fear, of isolation, of abuse, of oppression, of physical pain, of emotional hurt, of mental anguish?

What if we offered space to lift these experiences of loss not just intentionally in Lent but intentionally the entire liturgical year? And what would happen if we broke the taboo of not singing our alleluias during Lent?

If we are people of the gospel, of the *euangelion* (the good news), then Easter informs every element of who we are, regardless of the liturgical season in which we sit. In fact, it seems that Lent, the season in which we intentionally linger in the emotions and expressions of grief, mourning, guilt, and remorse, is perhaps the *perfect* time to be reminded of the essential news, the life-giving news that despair need not, will not, win. Hope, in other words, is present, even when it seems that it is exactly the absent thing.

I've come to decide that without being reminded through and through with Easter knowledge, Lent can feel like forty days of masochistic liturgical pain. We can't appreciate the import of the cross, regardless of whether it offers forgiveness and/or comfort and/or hope, if we don't know Easter.

The cross left alone is an announcement that death does win.

The cross left alone calls life a wrap—and via suffering, to boot.

The cross left alone gives no hope for Odes to Joy and leaves us only with Odes to Lament.

That's deeply unfortunate at best and deeply damaging at worst. A person needs at least an Ode to Hope to get us through our Lenten season(s). What is Easter if not a reason to sing an Ode to Hope, and does it not deserve an alleluia, even (especially?) during Lent?

My late mentor, Walt Bouman, spoke of how living the Christian life is like reading a mystery novel . . . starting with the last chapter first. If you read the last chapter first and *then* begin at the beginning, you enter the story differently. You learn what door, person, or dark alley to avoid; about what and whom you should or shouldn't care; and the degree to which you should be invested in either grief or joy. You might even know whether the book is worth the read.

Bouman's point (aside from being totally wrong about how we should read mystery literature) was that as Christians, we have, in essence, read the last chapter first. We know the end of the story. We know that, as I like to say, death is real but life is real-er. We know that Good Friday is a thing, and tears are a thing, and disillusionment is a thing, and loss is a thing, and grief and regret and fear and fatigue and lament are all things.

But we are different from the women at the tomb and the disciples at the cross. We are no different in our experiences of sorrow, of course, but we *are* different because we, in contrast to them on that awful Friday and Saturday, know that Jesus did not stay dead. We have read the last chapter.

That doesn't negate that sometimes we still open the wrong doors, get attached to the wrong people, and suffer the death of others—and, always looming, our own. But it does negate the purported final triumph of the loss, the regret, the anger, the emptiness, and the pain.

I think that rather than inviting people to ignore their negative experiences during this season, by framing Lent (or any season of life touched by grief) with Easter and lacing it through with some alleluias—even through our tears—we welcome people all the more to *feel* the negative experiences that make the alleluias all the more poignant and welcome and necessary. At the same time, I believe we also validate these events and emotions.

Lament names a wide swath of regret, grief, and suffering. In it we acknowledge them, we honor them, and we stand with those who feel them. You see, God did not intend people to suffer or to mourn, and certainly not alone. A person wouldn't know that, however, if a person didn't know Easter. Death *would* be God's Last Word. That cross on our Wednesday foreheads *would* be all we need because that would be the final truth.

However, the event of the cross is one bracket on some holy three days: Easter frames the other end of the Paschal Triduum. We need both, for both are true. Without the cross, Easter is superfluous. And without Easter, the cross is victor. And without Lent, without lament, we have no community to engage in two sacred acts: to acknowledge and wipe away our tears of grief, of mourning, and (of course) of sinfulness, and to sing us into (and perhaps, for a spell, sing on our behalf) hopeful alleluias nevertheless and in the in-between times of our lives.

Lent, in other words, is not just a season, and lament is not constrained to Lent.

They're life.

Lament and Remembrance

Liturgy is, in fact, a communal act of remembrance. It gathers the people of God together to recall our shared history, our shared promises, and our shared hope.

Pastor Dominique DuBois Gilliard, director of Racial Righteousness and Reconciliation for the Love Mercy Do Justice Initiative of the Evangelical Covenant Church, believes that although lamentation "feels inherently ancient, . . . lamentation is a powerful act, one the church desperately needs to reclaim.

In our world of non-stop news and social media, lamentation is an essential and even revolutionary act. . . . When we lament, we confess our humanity." Lamentation, he says, "requires four steps: remembrance, reflection, confession, and repentance."[26]

It isn't a far distance from what the ancient Hebrews felt: memory connected them to the pain and yet also to the rescue of their forebears. But the invitation is to reflect upon the way in which we not only participate in our own suffering but also recall the suffering of others. We are then primed to confess our role not only in our pain but in the pain giving rise to lament that others experience, and we are given the courage to repent of it.[27]

In his 1986 Nobel lecture, "Hope, Despair and Memory," the late Jewish Holocaust survivor and author Elie Wiesel wrote that "remembering is a noble and necessary act. The call of memory, the call to memory, reaches us from the very dawn of history. No commandment figures so frequently, so insistently, in the Bible. It is incumbent upon us to remember the good we have received, and the evil we have suffered."[28]

Wiesel survived the Holocaust and consequently served all of humanity as an author, a Nobel laureate, and an incessant siren to the collective responsibility of remembrance. His words excerpted above are but one small sample of his abundant teaching about the necessity of recollection, of telling the stories of oppression and injustice so that their horror and their truth won't happen again. "*It is incumbent upon us to remember the good we have received, and the evil we have suffered.*" Incumbent— that's a significant word. We have no choice but to remember. It is a command, a calling, a credo: remember and tell.

Shortly after Wiesel died in 2016, I read an article by Rev. Dr. William Flippin in *Living Lutheran* entitled "Grounded in Grace: You Visited Me."[29] It's geared toward the call to visit those in prison and is based on this passage from Hebrews 13:3:

"Remember those who are in prison, as though you were in prison with them; those who are being tortured, as though you yourselves were being tortured." In his article, Rev. Dr. Flippin writes, "Remember is a serious word, for it calls for more than just occasionally mentioning someone in prayer—it means behaving as if we, too, were in danger of imprisonment." It's a participatory word, a word of solidarity, a word of companionship.

Especially since the rise of Black Lives Matter, it has become clear that white people will never comprehend Black people's constant fear and anger and frustration until we experience their oppression and deaths as our own. Thanks to Rev. Dr. Flippin, I hear this truth differently now: we won't understand unless we are behaving as if we, too, are in danger of imprisonment or of getting shot, if we too love someone whom we have long been told we must not, or if we too must flee oppression by crossing a border. By remembering the sufferings, we feel what the suffering ancestors have felt and what the sufferers among us now feel. Without this partnership in remembering, although white people can sing spirituals, it is questionable whether white people can understand why they are sung and, in fact, whether they should sing them at all.

But one can remember not just sufferings but what others did or did not do. Martin Luther King Jr. comes at remembrance from a different angle. He writes, "Darkness cannot drive out darkness; only light can do that. Hate cannot drive out hate; only love can do that. In the End, we will remember not the words of our enemies, but the silence of our friends. Life's most persistent and urgent question is, 'What are you doing for others?'"[30] That is, remembering also means calling to account those who harmed not only by way of action but by way of inaction. Remembering calls us to get in the streets, to call our legislators, to change our choices based on heretofore unrecognized privilege.

In this way, remembering is lament in motion.

For this reason, Walter Brueggemann believes that remembering is, at its root, all about hope. Hope, of course, is often yoked to the future, and this makes sense: I hope for all sorts of future things that may or may not come to pass. But Brueggemann suggests that hope is tied to the past and pulled into the future. Hope, he says, can be found in the recitation of events of despair and, still and even so, God's constancy in the midst of it. If we return to the past—and not a whitewashed past but the honest past—we can see where death has been evident and new life bursts forth anyway. "An act of memory," says Brueggemann, "enables the speaker to look away from . . . defeat, in order to draw upon older, continuing resources."[31]

What are those older resources?

Texts.

Tradition.

Tales of God's continuing love and grace and mercy and attention to the Least of These.

To that end, Brueggemann writes this: "Every time a pastor and a choir director get together to pick hymns, the work is one of constructive imagination designed to lead the congregation in turn to imagine the world in a certain way. Much worship is informed by tradition and conventional practice, but those who construct such worship must each time commit an act of imagination in order to determine what is to be accented and to adapt the advocacy to the specificity of context."[32]

It's a beautiful passage. One can't help but notice how many times the word *imagine* and related phrases appear within it. "Constructive imagination," "to imagine the world," "an act of imagination," all reference the role and consequence of communal worship. Brueggemann believes that worship returns us to the raw and painful and yet occasional triumphal past to help us imagine, and even re-create, a new future that mirrors and captures and stewards the imprint of the reign of God.

As the *imago Dei*, we are perfectly primed to imagine God's promises anew.

In these latter days, we are collectively experiencing a crisis of conscience, of community, of re-collection. People of privilege have too long forgotten the daily and all-too-long reality of those who are oppressed, or to adapt Rev. Dr. Flippin's words, people of privilege have not often enough behaved in solidarity as if they too were oppressed.

Convenient amnesia, we could call it.

Those of us in the church have a shot at redeeming our bent toward convenient memory repression: worship. In worship, we gather as members—that is, we re-member—to partake in a body and blood that is of a very different essence: one of equity and welcome and safety and peace. In worship, we re-collect our identity found in text after text, tale after tale, teaching after teaching that tells of a society where the proud are scattered, the hungry are filled, the lowly are raised, and God remembers God's mercy.

Gilliard's four ways to lament—remembrance, reflection, confession, and repentance—sound an awful lot like liturgy. Remembrance and reflection are found in the rereading of Scripture, listening to the sermon, and confessing our sins, and then, as we leave the service, we have been cleansed and called to repent and sent to serve and live anew.

Perhaps lament has been latently in there all along.

We just need to call a thing what it is a little louder.

Remembrance is increasingly taking place through acknowledgment of the Indigenous land upon which worship and other gatherings are taking place. My first experience with this practice was in Camrose, Alberta, Canada, at a synod assembly at which I was presenting. The blessing went like this:

We are a people called and gathered and washed.

We stand on sacred ground.

We acknowledge that the land on which we gather is Treaty 6 territory and a traditional meeting ground for many Indigenous peoples.

The territory on which the Augustana Campus of the University of Alberta is located provided a traveling route and home to the Cree, Blackfoot, and Métis, as it did for the Nakoda, Tsui T'ina, Chipewyan, and other Indigenous peoples. Their spiritual and practical relationships to the land create a rich heritage for all who gather here.

Twice the above words were read: once in the chapel prior to opening worship and once in the main gathering hall, at each of the inaugural events in these two separate places of communal gathering. It's a stunning, humbling acknowledgment of the history of these spaces and places, for without this public remembrance, worship and decisions and gathering and thinking and conversing would go down with no recognition of this land's sacred past and present meaning, and its meaning- and memory-laden past would remain forgotten. The synod has come to see that those who loved and love this place as theirs, who mourn its loss, who remember it, are due these words as an act of repentance and respect.

Likewise, a few years ago, daughter Else and I were driving down to Duluth. We passed by—as we do almost every time we buzz to Duluth and back—the site of a tragic accident that occurred several months before this particular day. I sighed and told her that as much as I miss Regensburg, Germany, where our family's life-changing accident occurred, I have been thankful many times over that we left when we did. I didn't and still don't think that I could bear going by the site of the accident that claimed so much. But, I said, other people pass there every day and don't even know that at that site, a life was taken and countless lives were changed. Just, I said, as streams of people will drive up and down the North Shore right on by the site that claimed a different life and changed so many others.

We talked, then, on the way to her school, about how every day, we all walk and drive and work and go to school where, sometime in the past, something happened that mattered to somebody. And generally, we are oblivious to the stories that the places could tell, could they speak.

The same thing happens with dates.

On June 19, 2004, an accident occurred that killed my husband and gave Karl the brain injury. That year, the next day, June 20, was Father's Day. Two days after that, June 22, is the anniversary of my late husband's and my ordination. And June 23 was my late husband's birthday. So compressed in a few days is more than a handful of history—grievous *and* joyous.

I've been reminded that every place and every day has meaning to someone. Be they occasions of deep grief, deep joy, or simply the familiar knowledge of a place one calls home, no moment and no place is untouched by the sacred memories created then and there. The synod assembly's intentional acknowledgment of place, of story, of loss, and of remembrance struck me powerfully. It's a spiritual practice, among other things.

And it left me wondering whether we could be, on a daily and interpersonal basis, similarly as mindful of significant, unheard lamentable stories that occurred in the places and in the people we encounter. That is, could worship and decisions and gathering and thinking and conversing intentionally recognize the sacred past and present meaning *of* that place and *for* those people to prevent their meaning- and memory-laden past from being tragically forgotten?

I can't help but imagine that, to use Wendell Berry's phrase, "a pattern of reminding," let alone a habit of remembering, might offer opportunities for compassion, for humility, for inquiry, for repentance, for renewal, for lament, for connection, not just to the present, but to the past, a reminder that we all—and that all that is—is connected, is sacred, is worthy of being told and heard and that we all have reason to lament, and to lament on behalf of one another.

In this way, lament can't help but lead to transformation.

Lament and Transformation

Gilliard believes it is impossible to lament in speed mode. Lament insists that we engage the pain. To mind it. To attend to it.

Why?

"Because," he says, "paradoxically, often the best way to cure pain is to engage it. Lamentation prevents us from becoming numb and apathetic to the pain of our world. . . . Lamentation begets revelation. It opens our eyes to death, injustice, and oppression we had not even noticed. It opens our ears to the sounds of torture, anguish, and weeping that are the white noise of our world. To live without lament is to live an unexamined life."[33] And, I believe, an untransformed life too.

As I've written about in a prior book,[34] I am concerned that, due to Luther's fight against indulgences, the Protestant grasp—especially the Lutheran grasp—of the gospel has been trained on the forgiveness of sins. The effect of that narrow understanding of the implications of the gospel has been that Christians have come to assume that the effects of the gospel are efficacious primarily for those who have sinned and for those who have died.

But the gospel, instead, is grounded in the event of Jesus's resurrection. That *euangelion* is still good news for us yet today because we are still today confronted with any manner of forms of death. God's future, as revealed to us in Jesus's resurrection, redefines our present.

West asserts that, via hard-won ways, Black theology has long understood that "the eschatological aspect of freedom in black Christianity is . . . neither a glib hope for a pie-in-the-sky heaven nor an apocalyptic aspiration that awaits world destruction. Rather, it is a hope-laden articulation of the tragic quality of everyday life of a culturally degraded, politically oppressed and racially coerced labor force. Black Christian eschatology is anchored in the tragic realism of the Old Testament wisdom literature and the proclamation of a coming kingdom by Jesus Christ."[35]

Faith in Jesus is savored, treasured, clung to not just because of the forgiveness of sins, as it tends to be in white Christian traditions, but rather for present and real relief from *all* manner of suffering. Hope for God's future injects not just expectation but palpable, practical hope into the hopeless now and reminds those who suffer that present pain is not a facet of God's agenda. It promises that God is in the midst of pain and grief with an eye not just to redemption to come but to immediate redemption and, yes, even judgment. The white church's tendency to focus on future heavenly relief allows Christians to avoid noticing crises immediately at hand, or lamenting them, or amending them.[36]

The traditional white church offers the platform for cheap grace.

But there are occasions when lament might be all that one can do. Death, relationships that are lost, illnesses, unwelcome—even the necessary ones—transitions, these grief-inducing experiences can be devastating, and nothing can be done, per se, not even hope, except to grieve. One can't act; one can only crumble.

It falls to those of us who witness the lament—who see and point to it (the Greek word for "witness" is *martyria*, from which we get, of course, "martyr")—to witness *to* the lament, advocating for relief from the suffering at hand.

When the Sandy Hook Elementary shooting occurred on December 14, 2012, it was all I could do to overrule my frantic compulsion to run down the street to my children's elementary school, situated far away from Newtown but not far away from me, and scoop them up to safety. That night, I held Karl and Else powerfully close. It was also all I could do to let them go to school the next day.

But when the unspeakable, unfathomable awfulness that descended upon Marjory Stoneman Douglas High School in Parkland, Florida, occurred a few years later on February 14, 2018, when one more shooter stole seventeen more lives of breath and stole joy and peace from all those who knew and loved them, I confess that I sighed and wiped tears from my eyes, and I continued to progress through my day.

And the next morning, post–school shooting, although I *thought* about the "what-if" of a shooter on the loose at their respective schools, nonetheless with relative confidence, I put my son on the bus, and I dropped my girl off, and then I moved on to the next thing.

So what was behind that sort of internal shift?

What was happening to me?

Was I acclimating myself to horror?

Was "another day, another shooting" now my new, accepted, and acceptable normal?

And should I feel guilty about the ease with which my children and I moved through our respective days after the news?

When I see the pictures of the parents wailing in grief, I remember in my soul—I know in my soul—what they now, ever so regrettably, know too.

When I learned that my husband was killed and that my son might not make it either—and if he did, he would be terribly, permanently wounded in unpredictable ways—the grief, the disbelief, the paralyzing shock was my first foray into apocalyptic living. Nothing seemed real, everything was hypervivid, and the emotions of despair and confusion and grief and desperation were so powerful as to be themselves *sur*real.

Those who had sung the song of lament before were surely singing a different tune out of their own tragic circumstances, but our voices were all united in the same key of grief.

The intensity of it all was absolutely unsustainable. It was impossible to feel all that I was feeling and simultaneously function. It had to, somehow, abate.

Trouble was, I felt as if abandoning my grief was abdicating the integrity of my pain.

Oddly, I felt somehow *loyal* to my pain. Laughing, picking up a latte, caring about, say, the Minnesota Twins standings in the league, all of that somehow felt horrifically disrespectful of my own pain, and that of my son's, and that of my daughter's. I feared that I'd rendered my crucial trauma as petty and the petty as crucial.

But then, suddenly, after a spell, I discovered . . . myself laughing, of all things, and latte-ing, and checking the baseball stats.

I also found myself breathing more and weeping less.

Suddenly, too, I became a better mama.

Pretty soon I found myself able to not just laugh, and latte, and stat check, but I had the energy and chutzpah again to advocate on behalf of those I'd never meet who were still—or would one day be—curled up in a ball, wrapped only in their own grief: the hungry, the forgotten, the exploited, the vulnerable.

Joy, you see, just like grief, is contagious.

The point is this: those who are afflicted cannot do anything but despair. They can barely breathe. It is a tragic holy space, and it is their calling to be in it. But the rest of us, we have a different space to inhabit, a different calling, for we are able to do something instead of despair.

We *have* to do something instead of despair, because they can't.

Their role is to lament.

That's it.

Lament.

Our role is to lament . . . *and.*

For if *everyone* laments, and if that's *all* that we do, then two terrible things happen:

First, nothing changes.

Nothing changes because our energies are taken up and sapped by grief. Nothing changes because we have no breath to resist the normalcy of enabled mass shooting after mass shooting after mass shooting and the incredibly powerful systems that are quite content to empower the gun lobby interests over the interests of keeping our babies safe. Nothing changes with racism, economic inequity, homelessness, fleeing refugees, sexism, LGBTQIA bigotry. Nothing changes because the death of our loved ones and the death of our grief claim the death of energy to do anything but weep.

Those who despair need those who can breathe to resist, in every possible way, the deadly trajectory of systems that not just tolerate but even, say, train for the deadly trajectories of bullets that spray in our schools and in our streets.

Second, despair wins.

I learned many things postaccident. One of them was this: when joy disappears, death wins again. That possibility ticked me off and was in part what moved me to do something as simple as care about the Minnesota Twins again. Because as real, as painfully, horribly, inexpressibly, terribly real as it is that these young people lost their lives, these things are equally real: Babies burp. Lakes shimmer. Music lilts. Lovers love. Puppies tumble.

Boys who were supposed to die learn to walk, bit by bit, again.

Girls without papas still learned to drive, to mow, to use power tools (that is not my strong suit), to know which guys need to be told au revoir (that is my strong suit).

See, death wants us to forget the truth of joy. Those who are dead but technically alive have forgotten these truths. No blame there to be had. But we who are alive, or we who are coming into life again, despite death and to spite death, we recall, we begin to recall, and when the time is right, we can remind.

I learned, then, what I have come to call the Art of Joyful Defiance.

We must defy death by defying it not least of all with joy. There is no reason, you see, for devastated people to move beyond their devastation if there is nothing beyond it.

We who are not crumpled by grief are freed to be reminders of, ambassadors of joy, of the possibility that there will be a day when even a small smile *will* creep against the sides of the mouth.

We who are not crumpled by grief are freed to be reminders of, ambassadors of, tangible hope that things will not stay as they were.

We who are not crumpled by grief are freed to be reminders of, ambassadors of, a normalcy that does not include inexpressible, existential pain.

Truth be told, if we all fully appreciated the entire pain of the world, none of us would get up off the floor. Let us not forget that the word *despair* means, quite literally, "to have no hope."

We who have breath not only know to hope: we can breathe it into those who, for the moment and perhaps for long days and months and years of moments, have none.

The wrong, then, the dishonor, the disrespect, is not in laughing, or latte-ing, or Minnesota Twins-ing it again. The wrong, the dishonor, the disrespect is *only* doing that.

Steward the pain, then, by changing the world for the better on behalf of those who cannot. Steward the joy by creating a world where those who mourn have reason to breathe, reason to come back to life, reason maybe even to smile while drinking a latte (and/or a very fine red—I recommend Cooper & Thief myself) and checking the stats.

Lament and Redemption

Elie Wiesel wrote a newspaper article in 2000 that I have on my wall in my study. It's *auf Deutsch* because it appeared in the German newspaper *Die Zeit*. The theme of the article is "I Have a Dream." It was a series in which various people known for one thing or another were invited to reflect on those words. Wiesel wrote about some of his dreams and how, while in the camps, he would dream of his younger years, before the "Reign of the Night," times that were filled with joy and innocence. But then he writes this: "Zurzeit träume ich nicht mehr vom Messias. Er besucht meine Träume nicht mehr. Er kam nicht, als er erwartet wurde. Also hat er Verspätung. Macht nichts, der Jude in mir wartet weiter auf ihn."[37]

The translation: "These days I don't dream any more of the Messiah. He doesn't visit my dreams anymore. He didn't come when he was expected. Fine. Something must have held him up. He's late. Doesn't matter. The Jew in me will continue to wait for him."

I've often said that before I'd suffered, I loved the song "Soon and Very Soon": "Soon and very soon, we're gonna see the King."

There's no more crying there, no more dying there.

I do love the tune. I dare anyone to not find oneself tapping their foot or humming it even hours after they've heard it. But after some suffering hit me, I found myself mulling, "What does 'soon' *mean*, exactly?" It's been a spell since Jesus was here, and

I'm beginning to be curious about the actual metric by which we *measure* "soon."

Soon in dog years? Soon as in a metaview of history? Because sometimes, in the midst of suffering, soon feels like an eternity. A lot of *Scheisse* has happened since the first century, that is. Heck, even today's *news*, regardless of what your today was, told of a lot of *Scheisse* that has happened.

Think of when you have the stomach flu. You feel miserable. Then you hear "You'll feel better *soon*—just a couple of days of this and you'll be fine," and you want to die before you slog through two more days of the uck.

Or when you've lost a love, a loved one, a dream, trust: "You'll get over it soon." Or even now, the end of Covid can't come soon enough.

My Jewish friend Murray asks, "If Jesus is the redeemer, where is the redemption?" His question haunts me. And it makes me wonder, by what metric, actually, do we, should we, can we measure redemption?

So I find that I stand with the Jews who are still waiting for the Messiah, as do all Christians through Good Friday and through Holy Saturday, and stalwartly so. But we still hope, and then trust, in Easter.

This crazy story, this tale of a man who embraced the least of these; who hung out with, as Bruce Cockburn sings so elegantly in "Cry of a Tiny Babe," "shepherds and street people, hookers and bums"; who raised glasses of the best wine and shared food with any he could; who healed and forgave and called out the powerful and decried the hypocrisy of the religious and political leaders but who loved his Jewish tradition mightily and saw himself as faithful to it; and who was killed because of his fidelity to a vision of justice and equity and mercy and wholeness—this entire shebang has a grip on me like no other.

I understand the fear of those who wanted to be loyal to him but were not. I understand the eventual betrayal of those who loved him and who did love him but were still bound by self-protection. I understand the grief that was felt by those who betrayed him and by those, like the women, who did not. I understand the uncertainty that filled their very bones, now that everything that they had thought to be true about Jesus and about themselves was apparently not. And I understand the joy when they realized that they were right, but not at all in the way they thought they were.

Their betrayal and grief and uncertainty were real, that is. But I can't help but believe that resurrection is real-er. There is no doubt that things are not as they should be. And there is no doubt that they are not as God thinks they should be: we have a long scriptural tradition that tells us that God's vision for the world is very much what the world is not.

But the resurrection gives us a revelation not just of what God's vision is but of our invitation to be part of it, an invitation that we all too often refuse because we are afraid: we are afraid of the implications of our loyalty, of the implications of our betrayal, of the implications of our grief, of the implications of our disoriented sense of what is real and what is not, of the implications of faithful living that could—and if we do it right almost certainly will—lead to our death in one form or another.

That is, the resurrection informs us that God's vision for us, God's agenda for us, God's invitation to us is *life* and that anything that stands in the way of it no longer is ultimate.

Life is more powerful than death.

One morning, I told Karl that he reminds me of Easter all the time: he was supposed to die, I said. And then Karl grinned and said in his slow, determined speech, "But I *didn't*!" And then went straight to his favorite Monty Python line: "I'm not dead yet!" I just about died right then and there by way of grateful laughter for my son.

I don't know when God's reign in its fullness will come. But I have come to see resurrection, this defiant rejection of death and grief and despair, take place in real time, this "joyful defiance" or "tangible Easter," again and again and again and again.

And what has gotten me through the darkest of days are questions . . . and answers . . . born out of the cross and born out of the resurrection.

"Why have you forsaken me?" I have cried.

"I have not," God's replied.

"Where is God?" I have cried.

"I'm right here," God's replied.

And when I see death come my way, or in the way of those who deserve no harm, by way of actual death, or fear, or fatigue, or illness, or injuries, or injustice, or even just the taxing encounters of pettiness or the exhausting realities of adulting or the ridiculousness of the power plays of those who hold temporary political power, I rise up.

I rise up. I do.

I rise up because I see death trying to tell me that it is coming for me and that I should succumb to its power, and that torques me off. It torques me off because death is not the way of God. I know this because if it were, Jesus would still be dead.

It torques me off because it lies, manipulating me by telling me that I shouldn't own my grief, own my loss, own my fear, because to do so is to admit weakness and doubt in God. I know this because Jesus cried out from the cross and lived to see another day.

It torques me off because I can see how death entices me to tremble. But I know that there is nothing I need to ultimately fear anymore, especially death, because Jesus is risen.

It torques me off because death shows its power and says that there is no way for righteousness to win. But I know that that's exactly how death gains its power but that, in fact, it's already lost it.

It torques me off because death has already taken so much, and I refuse to cede death another win.

I refuse.

In the name of God, and God help me, I will not give it that satisfaction. I know that death has a word but is no longer the last one. I am freed to give death the raspberries and carry on.

It is true that I may, on any given day, have a Jew in me, *die Jüdin die immer noch auf den Messias warte*. And it is true that on any given day, I may not know what "soon and very soon" means, and I am not entirely sure that God does either.

But I do know what hope means.

And I do know what defiance means.

And I do know what resurrection means.

And I do know what joy means.

It means that death is real.

And in spite of and to spite that truth, Life. Is. Real-er.

Joy Comes in the Mourning

Kitsch annoys me. I don't just have a low-kitsch level; I have a no-kitsch level. My personal moratorium on kitsch is true in all cases and for all times, excepting kitsch that is so bad, it is good. The trick, of course, is identifying what constitutes kitsch. Kitsch as a *concept* is hard to explain, but you know it when you see it.

I myself have two archetypal examples of kitsch here in my home, and they both have places of honor: one on my window shelf in my study, and another comes out only once a year and hangs in a position of prestige on our Christmas tree. Both were gifts. Neither would I ever, ever, ever, ever, ever have purchased for myself.

One has every single religious reference you could possibly consolidate on a small surface. It's an egg, actually, a really big ostrich egg with the Lord's Prayer written on fake parchment with burned edges on the back and Jesus praying in the Garden of Gethsemane on the front, both shellacked to the surface; a hidden button on the bottom that plays "Amazing Grace"; and a door with a golden betasseled pull string that opens to plastic praying hands set upon a pedestal of pastel flowers. The whole thing is arrayed in varnished baby-blue paint, the egg itself on a pedestal, arrayed with golden ribbons and a plastic gold and bejeweled cupola topper that is itself about an inch and a half tall.

The second is a significantly large Styrofoam sphere, completely wrapped in a cream-colored, shiny, silky thread, the strands of which meet at the bottom of the ball and are collected into an eight-inch dangling tassel, itself pulled together in several bulbous clumps with golden thread. The ornament is festooned with long needles pressed in toward the center, leaving only their glued-on fake pearls to be seen in a precise, symmetrical pattern, interrupted only by a(nother) glued-to-the-surface shellacked nativity scene framed by a metallic gold-colored ribbon, with a long textured golden loop at the top to drape the ornament onto, every single year, one of the most prominent branches of our tree.

Our family's decorating style is somewhere in the warm Scandinavian / cozy Northern Woods zone, and while it's always cluttered with laundry and books and mail and the Stuff of Life, we are otherwise fairly . . . simple. Streamlined. So the musical spinning egg and the gold and shiny ornament are decor anomalies, shall we say, from our typical tastes.

Nonetheless, they were each gifted with great sincerity and love, and so we sincerely love them back and smile when our eyes fall on them, admiring both the love behind them and the glop on them.

As art, though, how to put this . . . there's a lot going on there. Each piece is positively over the top, gaudy even, heavy with baubles and shine and ribbons and gold and sound and religiosity, and my eyes and mind are somewhat overwhelmed by it all. You need to intentionally set aside some time and emotional energy to take it all in.

But it's exactly these two pieces that came to mind as the symbolic representation of why, of all the topics that would claim my attention, joy is not the go-to even *I* would expect. In fact, I've long had a problem with joy, and to be honest, this book was one means to figure out what it was and why.

This much I knew: at face value, joy feels kitschy to me.

Saccharine.

Fluffy.

Compulsory gladness.

And I think I come by this feeling honestly, from not least of all being steeped in the Christian tradition, which is, I think, steeped in a notion of joy that is at base superficial. With all due respect to the noble and worthy traditional camping system, the song "Joy in My Heart"—"I've got the joy joy joy joy / down in my heart. (Where?) / Down in my heart. (Where?) / Down in my heart / I've got the joy joy joy joy / down in my heart. Down in my heart to stay"—makes me break out in hives.

I think it's because I know what many readers of this book know—namely, that life is not always joyful. In fact, sometimes it's excruciatingly painful.

Sometimes it's stressful.

Sometimes it's overwhelming.

And sometimes it's simply boring.

To be joyful all the time, to be expected to be joyful all the time, to have the joy down in my heart to stay forever and always seems like both a bit much to live up to and also a bit Pollyanna-esque. For all these reasons, the "Life Is Good" apparel line—or even just the phrase—always gets a bit of the stink eye from me: life is not *always* good, and to pretend it is glosses over or even outright ignores real pain, real loss, and real grief, if not yours, then that of someone who comes upon you wearing that shirt.

It might sound as if the only thing I ought to add is "Bah humbug to joy," but, in fact, I'm not opposed to joy! Rather, my allergic reaction to obligatory joy stems in part to wondering, How can one be joyful—in fact, *can* one be joyful—if one has even a smidgen of awareness of the bleakness and grief that are present in the world and even our complicity in them, let alone in our lives?

Joy seems as if it is to be a full-bodied, through-and-through, transformational thing, and therefore, what? Unattainable even? But joy is, of course, a thing. It must be possible to experience joy, for if it weren't, we'd have no word for it, nor people who say that they know joy. To jump ahead, then, through the course of mulling and researching and writing this book, I've come to believe that joy is less a feeling and more a way of being.

Happy is an emotion.

Glad is an emotion.

But joy is somehow more *essential* than that—*essential* coming from the Latin word meaning "being." It is tied not just to a moment but to a way of encountering the world, one that wells up from a distinct posture toward the universe, one that shapes one's perspective of engaging life, and one that, for Christians, is utterly informed by the gospel that Jesus is risen.

———

Word nerd that I am, it took but a nanosecond, as I settled in to write this book, to look up the etymology of the word *joy*. Here's what I learned: The word *joy* comes from the Old French *joie*, which means "pleasure, delight, and bliss." That word in turn comes from the Latin word *gaudia*, which means the same: "joy, delight." And both in turn come from the proto-Indo-European root *gau-*, which means "to rejoice."

So joy comes, basically, from the root words meaning joy, news for which no one needs to be sitting to hear. But then, straightaway, I noticed, "Hold on: *gaudia* . . . gaudy . . ." Sure enough, the root word for *joy* is the same root word for *gaudy*! My joy-histamines were etymologically validated!

But wait, there's more! I poked around at the word *kitschy*, which comes from the German *Kitsch*, which itself is related to— wait for it—*gaudia*, the same root for both joy and gaudy! So my

Spidey-etymology senses were totally on fire for all the right reasons. Joy is, at least in its word history, related to the gaudy and the kitschy. No wonder I get a little squirmy and squeamish about it.

And yet, again, joy at its best, at its fullest, in its essence must mean, has to mean, please let it mean, something more than that of the tacky, the over the top, the gloppy.

Card tip: it does.

In seminary, I learned that it was faithfully possible to (1) be annoyed with Scripture and (2) be annoyed by forced happiness. It was Walter Brueggemann's book *Israel's Praise* that freed me to be both. About midway through, it became apparent that Brueggemann—Old Testament scholar *Walter Brueggemann!*—can't stand Psalm 150. It's beyond his capacity. He. Can. Not. Stand. Psalm 150.

Even if you don't recall offhand how Psalm 150 (RSV) goes, this last Psalm of them all, you may well as soon as you hear its first two lines:

> *Praise the Lord!*
> *Praise God in his sanctuary;*
> *   praise him in his mighty firmament!*
> *Praise him for his mighty deeds;*
> *   praise him according to his exceeding greatness!*
>
> *Praise him with trumpet sound;*
> *   praise him with lute and harp!*
> *Praise him with timbrel and dance;*
> *   praise him with strings and pipe!*
> *Praise him with sounding cymbals;*
> *   praise him with loud clashing cymbals!*

Let everything that breathes praise the Lord!
[And once more for good measure]
Praise the Lord!

Oh my *gosh* is that a lot of happiness. Maybe it's the introvert in me, but there is so much gold ribbon and silky tassels and pearl-topped pins and shellacked gladness in these verses, and I am looking for my joy-histamine Benadryl. And Brueggemann, this esteemed OT scholar, is all in with me. He writes,

> The world offered is absolute, presided over by an absolute God who has no history, no past, no future, no history of transformation.
>
> No reason is given for praise. No reason is given for the world over which Yahweh rules and in which Yahweh is to be praised. . . .
>
> This psalm assumes that everybody will praise, and no one will ask why. And if one asks why praise, the imperatives are received again with nonnegotiable authority and without reason. The God offered here with the accompanying "world" is absolute, without memory, without experience, without cause, simply a given that must be received and enacted. The world of doxology is solidly in place, but the old, embarrassing, revolutionary grounding for such a world has been eliminated.[1]

That last line is the kicker: in this psalm, "the world of doxology is solidly in place, but the old, embarrassing, revolutionary grounding for such a world has been eliminated." In other words, if you aren't willing to remember, to acknowledge, and even to protest evil, suffering, inequity, despair, and death, then you can't really know joy.

What you are experiencing is many things, but it isn't joy.

Whatever it is, though and therefore, is gaudy.

Kitschy.

But your *esse* remains untouched.

––––––

In the last chapter, I quoted the Heidelberg Disputation, in which Luther mentioned a "theologian of the cross" in distinction to a "theologian of glory." Now, as much as we hear the phrase "a *theology* of the cross," the truth is, Luther himself never used it. Instead, Luther wrote about a *theologian* of the cross, a truth that makes every theologian paying attention gulp. It's worth taking another look at these specific theses from another angle. Hear Luther: "That person does not deserve to be called a theologian who looks upon the invisible things of God as though they were clearly perceptible in those things which have actually happened."

In other words, don't be too big for your theological britches. It is haughty beyond measure to assume that you can most certainly see God, when in fact God most certainly works in mysterious ways, to use a tired term that still makes the point. You run into huge dangers here, Luther warned, because when you think you are seeing God's agenda, you might instead be seeing your own— and worse, baptizing it. Luther goes on: "He [argh] deserves to be called a theologian, however, who comprehends the visible and manifest things of God seen through suffering and the cross."

Only trust theologians, Luther says, who are able to perceive God where wailing can be heard and who know that there and there alone can we be sure that God is stirring, for God is a God who brings life out of death: "A theologian of glory calls evil good and good evil. A theologian of the cross calls the thing what it actually is."[2]

That right there is the key. A theologian of the cross calls the thing what it actually is. A theologian of glory, Luther says, will point to riches and security and a worry-free, very happy life and say, "I am so blessed! God loves me! Life is good!" But a theologian of the cross, in contrast, will look to that and say, "Get behind me, Satan."

Following Jesus—and, for that matter, Yahweh, as we see in the First Testament prophets whom Jesus called his own—means rejecting riches, rejecting security, rejecting the Good Life, and instead hobnobbing with the poor, embracing fidelity to God over fierce self-preservation, and entering a faithful life rather than the mere Good one.

Ever so slyly, you see, Luther was indicting much of his contemporary theological milieu—and presciently much of ours too—not to mention his pope, who by offering people a slip of paper, promised that they or their loved ones would spend less time in purgatory if they just ponied up more *Pfennige* now. Pope Leo was giving the faithful something tangible, something "clearly perceptible," as if the indulgences that they could tuck into their *Beutel* evidenced proof of the "invisible things of God" and, in fact, the reason for joy.

But that's not how it works, said Luther. We can never be quite sure of God's presence—and by this he meant God's affirmation of an event as blessed and holy—unless we are looking at suffering. Only where there is pain and only where there is grief can we be sure that God is at work, rather than *our* works at work, to bring about something redemptive, an agenda other than the one at hand, because God is nothing if not the bearer of hope and the one who turns mourning into joy.

If you see death, said Luther, if you see suffering, if you see *Anfechtung*—profound uncertainty and despair—if everything else is unsure, you can be sure of one thing: in these desperate moments, you also see God.

And here we detect a flicker of promise that joy is in the offing.

Why?

Because God is in the business of redemption, of making things new. But before we go one step further, we must note that this claim can have troubling extrapolations and be dangerously misunderstood.

Womanist, feminist, gay, Black, and liberation theologies, among many other theological approaches that are nonwhite and/or non–cis male, have many crucial issues with this approach. The idea that God is most certainly present when there is suffering raises several disturbing questions, like, Does one stay in an abusive marriage because God is apparently there? Do we tolerate, even condone, suffering because God must will it? Do we accept depression and the deprivation of delight as being somehow ordained—or at the very least preferred—by God?

These critiques have powerful and valid traction. In fact, much of Christian tradition has distorted the dogma that God is present in suffering, or wills it, as is evidenced by incidents of self-maceration, self-starvation, self-isolation, self-deprivation, self-loathing, and when looking at pain and inequity that can be found in the world, a mere shrug is offered in response.

Laced throughout this book and in my earlier book, I address this warped understanding of the conviction that God is present in suffering. For the moment, though, we'll harness our attention to Luther's *intended* point, because his insight, when taken a different direction, has traction too. To understand why it does, it's essential to remember what Luther here was implicitly attacking: the idea that God is a God who can be placated by bribes of praise and that God is a God who rewards those who, in any number of ways, buy this God off.

A theologian of glory is all about praise, period. A theologian of glory trusts that worldly success and blithe happiness are signs of God's approval. But a theologian of the *cross* instead is all about *passion*—passion, here, in the sense of suffering (*passio*) engagement with the world.

A theologian of the cross trusts that out of death comes resurrection.

Perhaps paradoxically at first, it is here, you see, that a theology of the cross can birth a theology not of glory and not of cheap grace but of joy. At this point, a key excursus on resurrection and the cross is necessary, because it is here we can build a framework of joy.[3]

Christians identify themselves as such because, along with the early followers of the risen Jesus, we believe that Jesus did not stay dead. We believe that he was raised from the dead, not least of all because it was women—despite women in that time and culture (and all too often still today) having had no power, no say, no trust, and no status at all—to whom the gospels attribute the initial proclamation of the resurrection! It was a very unwise rhetorical tactic . . . unless it's true.

Jesus's resurrection, revealed to women and told of by women and men, Jew and Gentile alike, confirmed that Jesus was indeed the Messiah of God, the One who had been awaited.

But the one who was awaited, the one who was raised, was someone specific, and the specific one was named Jesus. And this one, this Jesus, had a compulsion to feed, welcome, forgive, heal, and in various and sundry ways, enter into bleakness and bring about hope.

Relief.

Joy.

You see, not only does resurrection tell us that death is not God's agenda; the life lived by the one who was raised does too. Jesus's life was spent rejecting death in all its forms, wherever he encountered it, and instead springing up life to counter it.

Relatedly, every Christmas, we must endure the faux controversy about the abbreviation *Xmas* rather than the full-on, spelled-out *Christmas*. "Put the *Christ* back in *Christmas*," we begin hearing before it's even Advent. But of course, since the days of early Christianity, *X* was the symbol for Christ, as it is the first letter in the Greek spelling for Christ—Χρήστος (*Christos*).

As it is, I'm less concerned about putting *Christ* back in *Christmas* than I am about putting *Christ* back in *Christian*. Christians believe that Jesus—the one who healed, welcomed, fed the hungry, hung out with outcasts, called out the wealthy elites and hypocrites, and stepped across egregious boundaries—is the Christ. What he did is what we who claim his name are called to do too. It's a piece too often overlooked, especially in recent days, which is why all year long, and not just in the days surrounding the holidays, I'm of the mind that it's time to put the *Christ* back in *Christian*.

And when we do, we begin to experience a sense of joy, the sort one feels when one has been a vehicle for healing, and welcome, and feeding, and friending, and justice seeking and justice making, and bridge building. It is precisely *this* that Luther was attempting to say; it is *here* that Luther finds a rich and deep well into which he can dip and that one considering joy can dip into too.

In the bleakness of Good Friday, in the sources of lament, God began to get to work to resurrect hope and, ultimately, joy. A theologian of glory does not notice, prefers not to be troubled by, and opts not to care about suffering. A theologian of the cross, though, *does* notice, *is* troubled by, *does* care about suffering and, in the very name of the God who raised the dead, *ushers in hope and joy into the mix.*

And *this* is precisely what Brueggemann was attempting to say about his absolute eye-rolling at Psalm 150. It ignores the strife. There is no acknowledgment that it could be otherwise.

And to be very honest, his allergic reaction to Psalm 150 is the very same as my allergic reaction to much of contemporary praise music: it ignores the pain.

"Life is good" ignores that life can be bad. A psalter that takes out lament ignores the grief. Everything is not awesome. Luther's theology of the cross knows this to be true but also knows that if God gets to work where there is sorrow and despair, that also means that sorrow and despair are not God's intention for the world. There must be a place, must be room, must be righteousness in joy!

One of my favorite biblical words is *tzedek*. I first learned of it when I read a vignette by the late Lutheran theologian Joseph Sittler, who told of a time when he was traveling in Jerusalem, hit a pothole, and had to bring his car in to the mechanic. After the car had been repaired, Sittler was told that his car was *tzedek* again. This delighted Sittler to no end because when used in Scripture, the Hebrew word *tzedek* means "righteous"! If you are righteous, if you are *tzedek*, you are properly aligned to the Holy.

We know who and what the Holy is when we remind ourselves of who God is. So as mentioned earlier, Jesus healed and forgave and fed and welcomed and so forth. But Jesus also loved joy. For example, Jesus loved wine! Really good wine—though I'm sure that some textual analysis would suggest that at least on a few occasions, it actually says Danish akvavit.

And Jesus loved wine and food in community! Can you imagine the delight the hungry felt when they were fed and the delight of the disciples seeing that they had been ambassadors of delight by doling out the bread and the fish?

And Jesus loved studying: when Jesus was a young man, he stayed in the temple and taught. Never mind for a moment that he terrified his mother—the *point* is that he delighted in learning and teaching.

And Jesus loved rest—soothing, sabbath-like rest. Luther noted this tendency of Jesus, and Luther himself found profound joy and delight in his wife, and his children, and his music, and

his wife's beer. Luther did because he saw them as both exten-
sions of God's intentions and in counterdistinction from what
could in fact be—and was, for him, in multiple ways—quite
otherwise.

So Brueggemann does not like Psalm 150. But he does like
Psalm 103. About it he writes,

> The biblical community knows about the pain which needs no
> theoretical justification. It knows it is simply there. It lingers
> there relentlessly, silently, heavily. Moreover, the biblical com-
> munity knows the pain cannot be handled alone. In isolation,
> the power of pain grows more ominous and more hurtful. The
> pain must be handled in community, even if a community of
> only a few who will attend. It knows that finally pain must be
> submitted to the power of the holy God
>
> > *who forgives all your iniquity,*
> > *who heals all your diseases,*
> > *who redeems your life from the Pit,*
> > *who crowns you with steadfast love and mercy,*
> > *who satisfies you with good . . .*
> > *[who] works vindication . . . for all who are oppressed.*
> > (Ps 103:3–6)[4]

In other words, we know while experiencing pain that we can
expect joy because we have seen God do it before: bring life out
of death.

But Brueggemann goes further and even goes all-out
theology-of-the-cross on us. The history of redemption matters
powerfully in the psalms, he says. In the psalms of praise that
he *can* bear, Brueggemann sees a pattern that shows the God of
transformation, who once was angry or seemed absent, offering
mercy and being present. As he writes, "Then comes favor from

the God who has been angry, then comes a joy after weeping tarried in the night. There has been a transformation."[5]

Looking to Psalm 30 as an example, Brueggemann writes, "The more the [personal] transformation is reflected upon, the more inexplicable and wondrous it is; the more the turn wrought by God looms with cosmic significance. The transformation becomes a way to think about God's way elsewhere in the world, and Israel takes the change as a paradigm for God's characteristic way in the world."[6]

Again, God does not have an ironclad plan for the world but rather has a vision, an agenda for the world, and it is that of life, shalom, and joy. So using Psalms 30, 40, and 66 and even Jonah 2 as reference points, Brueggemann says that they express

> a sequence from trouble to complaint to divine intervention to a responding thanksgiving. They express a history of trouble turned to joy. Each time they are sung, they invite Israel to participate in that entire history of transformation again. The practice of the history of transformation guards against an idolatry of a god who cannot be changed and an ideology that imagines the world is fixed and settled. The song of thanksgiving characteristically avoids the temptations to idolatry and ideology to which the hymn is susceptible, because it has memory and hope which always stays close to pain and rescue.[7]

We see grief and joy intertwining also in Luke 1:46–55:

And Mary said,

> *"My soul magnifies the Lord,*
> *and my spirit rejoices in God my Savior,*
> *for he has looked with favor on the lowliness of his servant.*
> *Surely, from now on all generations will call me blessed;*

for the Mighty One has done great things for me,
   and holy is his name.
His mercy is for those who fear him
   from generation to generation.
He has shown strength with his arm;
   he has scattered the proud in the thoughts of their hearts.
He has brought down the powerful from their thrones,
   and lifted up the lowly;
he has filled the hungry with good things,
   and sent the rich away empty.
He has helped his servant Israel,
   in remembrance of his mercy,
according to the promise he made to our ancestors,
   to Abraham and to his descendants forever."

And in Luke 7:22: "And he answered them, 'Go and tell John what you have seen and heard: the blind receive their sight, the lame walk, the lepers are cleansed, the deaf hear, the dead are raised, the poor have good news brought to them.'"

Just as Mary knew—and Jesus wanted all to know—joy separate from grief and its transformation is not, in fact, joy. What's felt then is something else: a happy moment, a welcome distraction, a momentary relief, even a coping mechanism by way of avoidance. But the buoyant feeling anchored in the experience of the lament-worthy experiences of life is joy. That contrary way of being, says Brueggemann—namely, the maintenance of a forced smile at the cost of calling a thing what it is—is bull-pucky.

I do not know the Hebrew for "bull-pucky." But I do know that Israel's laments call such nonsense out. Israel knows what is possible by way of suffering because Israel has known death and displacement, and by way of joy, Israel has seen God's stirring of life in the midst of suffering. When Israel trusts in the God who sees suffering and death and overcomes them, rather than a God who pretends suffering and death do not exist or who wills them (i.e., a God espoused by a theologian of glory, a God who doles out cheap grace, a God who condones North American materialistic success), Israel recalls its history, Israel laments its present moment, and then it returns to thanksgiving and celebration.

In the healing of body or spirit or relationships, acts of justice, open feasts, generous welcomes, simple beauty, deep love, solid solidarity, remembering the forgotten . . . when such occasions take place, we see the trace of God. Our rebellion against that which stifles these expressions of holy redemption, thereby defying despair, let alone defying death, trusts that God is rebelling and defying despair and death with us (as God has done before).

Therein is cause for joy and are signs of hope that, in turn, cause more joy. In this way, you see, joy is not an emotion, not a passing feeling. Instead, it is a posture in life of defiance against that which is and should not be but finds delight and hope in that which is and should be—and, one day, will be for all.

Joy is an incarnate expression of salvation. And joy is a contagious invitation to a way of life that does not bend its being toward death but out of death bends its being toward life.

———

Joy dishwashing liquid.
The Joy of Sex.
Joie de vivre.
*Joy*ride.
The *joy*stick on my son's wheelchair.
Even *Schadenfreude*, which means "Joy at Misfortune."

Joy is a word that clearly can be put to many a use, though I am here to say that the dishwashing liquid people hit untapped—and arguably untappable—marketing gold when they associated joy with doing dishes. But unlike soap, there is no bottle of emotions that can simply, on demand, squirt out joy.

Joy can't simply be willed into being, despite what a culture enamored of the power of positive thinking might say. In an anecdote that gave rise to her book *Bright-Sided*, Barbara Ehrenreich tells of her daring foray into the culture of positive thinking on a Koman.org message board. In a post on a thread for breast cancer survivors, Ehrenreich lamented. She lamented the red tape of insurance companies, the unwelcome side effects of chemotherapy, and, as she says, "most daringly, 'sappy pink ribbons.'"

Her bravery was not rewarded. Instead, Ehrenreich was publicly excoriated for her lack of positivity, for her abundant bad attitude, and she was told, "Run, [do] not walk, to some counseling. Please, get yourself some help and I ask everyone on this site to pray for you so you can enjoy life to the fullest."[8]

Ehrenreich has opted to reflect on this almost coercive participation of positive thinking throughout *Bright-Sided*. And much like I have felt the need to do in this very book, Ehrenreich is also quite intent on convincing her readers that she is no curmudgeon:

> I would like to see more smiles, more laughter, more hugs, more happiness and, better yet, joy. In my own vision of utopia, there is not only more comfort, and security for everyone—better jobs, health care, and so forth—there are also more parties, festivities, and opportunities for dancing in the streets. Once our basic material needs are met—in my utopia, anyway—life becomes a perpetual celebration in which everyone has a talent to contribute. But we cannot levitate ourselves into that blessed condition by wishing it. We need to brace ourselves for a struggle against terrifying obstacles, both of our own making and

imposed by the natural world. And the first step is to recover from the mass delusion that is positive thinking.[9]

Joy, then, neither is the state of positive thinking nor can be willed into being by positive thinking. In fact, arguably, positive thinking undercuts the possibility of joy, because it refuses to give room to negative thinking, as the psalmists were wont to do. And similarly, joy is not happiness, just as despair is not the same as sadness. Like happiness, positive thinking is sustainable only for so long, taking intense emotional, even anxious, energy to maintain. And positive thinking, it turns out, does not always pan out. That leaves a person twice bowled over, first by way of the immediate loss and second by the betrayal of the trust so thoroughly given to the powers of positive thinking. It's not much different from the bewilderment felt when one believes (as a theologian of glory would) that God will save the situation, will heal the ill, will stop the death, and yet after all that, no prayed-for redemption comes.

The parable of King Midas—for that is what it is, a parable rather than a tale—reveals a different hard-won wisdom: joy cannot be possessed. Midas yearned for wealth. Money, he was convinced, would make his life complete. In an unfortunate way, he turned out to be right. An opportunity eventually arrived for him to test his theory. Silenus, a mentor to the Greek god Dionysus, had gotten lost in Midas's neighborhood. Midas, recognizing Silenus as no ordinary man, welcomed him and gave him safety. Dionysus, grateful for Midas's care of his dear friend, wished to reward him for his valiant hospitality and so struck on an idea: Midas could have whatever he wished.

It took Midas but a nanosecond to ask that everything he touched be turned to gold.

Glory be to Dionysus, it worked. It was a terrific deal. Midas's fingers magically transformed everything into glittering wealth. He could now die a wealthy man.

Now there are several versions of how this story ends. One is that he did just that: Midas died a wealthy man, albeit a starved one. Plates and goblets, along with the food and drink that they had once held, turned to gold as soon as he held them, and so Midas could not eat.

Another version is more wrenching: he hugged his daughter, who, of course, also turned to gold and died a glimmering statue.

Mihaly Csikszentmihalyi, author of *Flow: The Psychology of Optimal Experience*, studies what makes people content in life and what makes them feel unified within themselves and with their environments. What *doesn't* fulfill people are goals that are bound to external metrics.

If only Midas had read Csikszentmihalyi.

But Csikszentmihalyi has read about Midas. Using this tale, he's observed that people are often driven by that which is often called materialism, though their goals need not be tangible possessions such as money, fancy homes, nice cars, or even a lover. Instead, they can also be the more ephemeral, such as beauty, rank, power, prowess. Life becomes reduced to a pursuit of these idols but also, once acquired, to the maintenance of them, and the multiplication of them as well.

Not coincidentally, these are, as Csikszentmihalyi says, "all too powerful *symbols* of happiness."[10] The late theologian Paul Tillich would appreciate his use of "symbol" here, as Tillich believed that a sign points to something else, but a symbol does that *and* participates in that which is being pointed out. So money, beauty, status, and authority each represent an acquisition, but they are acquisitions as well. Those looking in from the outside see those who have all the apparent symbols of happiness as having happiness and being happy, and many covet the same.

If we had x, y, and z, *then* everything would be fine. But, says Csikszentmihalyi,

Symbols can be deceptive: they have a tendency to distract from the reality they are supposed to represent. And the reality is that the quality of life does not depend directly on what others think of us or on what we own. The bottom line is, rather, how we feel about ourselves and about what happens to us. To improve life one must improve the quality of experience.

This is not to say that money, physical fitness, or fame are irrelevant to happiness. They can be genuine blessings, but only if they help to make us feel better. Otherwise, they are at best neutral, at worst obstacles to a rewarding life.[11]

To some degree, Csikszentmihalyi describes the archetypal American pursuit, codified and canonized in our Declaration of Independence—namely, that "we hold these truths to be self-evident, that all men are created equal, that they are endowed by their Creator with certain unalienable Rights, that among these are Life, Liberty, and the pursuit of Happiness." United by and in a capitalistic framework, we certainly have the makings for individualistic pursuits of transient experiences of happiness, but not for the pursuit of joy. Joy, in fact, is not even pursue-able.

The Creator to whom these architects of America seemed to appeal would assuredly have a different understanding of Life, Liberty, and Happiness. Christianity is not particularly interested in happiness. Happiness as a word or a concept is not strong in New Testament writing, with the closest term perhaps being *makarios*, which is most often, as in the Beatitudes, translated as "blessed."

But happiness, certainly by the customary US standard, is simply not a Christian thing.

To make this even more manifest, German theologian Jürgen Moltmann has coined a term to describe our constant quest for entertainment: *Spaßgesellschaft*, a "fun society."[12] To be clear, he's not describing our culture as "fun"; he is saying that it, in a quite true sense, despairs for fun. We quest after fun until our need for fun is momentarily satiated. But fun, Moltmann believes, is sought after to distract us from the otherwise anxiousness, or banality, or grief of the ordinary days of life. It's also in stark contrast to joy, which instead "opens the soul, is a flow of spirits, giving our existence a certain easiness. We may *have* fun, but we *are* in joy."[13]

Not coincidentally, Moltmann is also unimpressed with the decision by the European Union to designate Beethoven's hymn "Ode to Joy" as its anthem. Not one for ambiguity or euphemism, Moltmann compares its lyrics to an opiate. The composition, Beethoven's well-known and well-loved Symphony no. 9 is based on Friedrich Schiller's poem after which the anthem is named. "Suffer on courageous millions / Suffer for a better world / O'er the tent of stars unfurl'd / God rewards you from the Heavens," sings the elegy.[14] After two horrific wars and the atrocities that led to them on European soil, Moltmann believes that the words are worthy of contempt, and the hymn is unworthy of the continent's history. People have and still do suffer unspeakable atrocities and despair, but the poem glosses over the agonies of this world. Instead, the poem focuses on otherworldly joy rather than this-worldly pain and protest.[15]

Moltmann, like Brueggemann, like West, like Ehrenreich, and, I hope, like myself, is no dour person, no grouch, no misanthrope. Instead, he too sees joy to be something far deeper than happiness and fun and far more bound to the lamentation of the lack of it; he sees the wedding of joy to justice seeking and creation loving rather than to some heavenly relief that shall come by and by. In fact, Christianity itself, he says, is a very "religion of joy." Moltmann points to Mary, whose spirit "rejoices in God" her Savior (Luke 1:46–47), and the angels' announcement of "good news of great joy" to the shepherds (Luke 2:10–11), and the joy of a risen Jesus, and the Pentecostal joy brought about by the Spirit of God. "Why then," he asks, "is Christianity such a unique religion of joy, even though at its center stands the suffering of God and the cross of Christ? Because we remember the death of Christ in the light of his resurrection, and we remember his resurrection in the splendor of the divine, eternal life that is embracing our human and mortal life already here and now."[16] Christian joy unites to persisting hope, not to passing happiness, transposing grief and suffering into an abiding sense of defiant, world-embracing, world-defining joy.

In this way, a Christian understanding of joy seems to involve participation in something beyond oneself. So, for example, Miroslav Volf picks up in Matthew 25 that the "good and trustworthy" servants were invited to "enter into the joy" of their master. He's struck by this phrase, finding it odd: you can enter into a house, into a space, into a family, which suggests that the object/place/relationship belongs to the one extending it. To enter into joy, though, implies that joy is itself not just offered from but stems from, is possessed by, and is shared through the Divine One.[17]

Volf finds this construct, this participatory joy held in relationship to God and others, in a number of New Testament places: in John 15:9–11 ("As the Father has loved me, so I have loved you; abide in my love. If you keep my commandments, you will abide in my love, just as I have kept my Father's commandments and abide in his love. I have said these things to you so that my joy may be in you, and that your joy may be complete."), Philippians 4:4 ("Rejoice in the Lord always; again I will say, rejoice."), and perhaps most sweepingly, Philippians 2:1–11:

> If then there is any encouragement in Christ, any consolation from love, any sharing in the Spirit, any compassion and sympathy, make my joy complete: be of the same mind, having the same love, being in full accord and of one mind. Do nothing

from selfish ambition or conceit, but in humility regard others as better than yourselves. Let each of you look not to your own interests, but to the interests of others. Let the same mind be in you that was in Christ Jesus,

> *who, though he was in the form of God,*
> > *did not regard equality with God*
> > *as something to be exploited,*
> *but emptied himself,*
> > *taking the form of a slave,*
> > *being born in human likeness.*
> *And being found in human form,*
> > *he humbled himself*
> > *and became obedient to the point of death—*
> > *even death on a cross.*

> *Therefore God also highly exalted him*
> > *and gave him the name*
> > *that is above every name,*
> *so that at the name of Jesus*
> > *every knee should bend,*
> > *in heaven and on earth and under the earth,*
> *and every tongue should confess*
> > *that Jesus Christ is Lord,*
> > *to the glory of God the Father.*

Each of these passages illustrates that Christian joy is deeply tied to community and communion with God. Indeed, the Greek word for joy, *chara*, carries the sense of gladness that is spiritually bound up in a way that connects the people, the context, delight, hope, and God. It's experienced as a gift and a mark of grace, as in Galatians 5:22–23 ("By contrast, the fruit of the Spirit is love, joy, peace, patience, kindness, generosity, faithfulness, gentleness, and self-control. There is no law against such things."); Acts 13:48–49, 52 ("When the Gentiles heard [that they would be told the gospel] they were glad and praised the word of the Lord; and as many as had been destined for eternal life became believers. Thus the word of the Lord spread throughout the region. . . . And the disciples were filled with joy and with the Holy Spirit."); and 1 Thessalonians 1:6–7 ("And you became imitators of us and of the Lord, for in spite of persecution you received the word with joy inspired by the Holy Spirit, so that you became an example to all the believers in Macedonia and in Achaia."), along with abundant references in the Farewell Discourse of John's Gospel, found in chapters 14–17.

But there are any number of additional expressions of joy, like those experienced during repentance, as proclaimed in Luke 15:7–10:

> Just so, I tell you, there will be more joy in heaven over one sinner who repents than over ninety-nine righteous persons who need no repentance.
>
> "Or what woman having ten silver coins, if she loses one of them, does not light a lamp, sweep the house, and search carefully until she finds it? When she has found it, she calls together her friends and neighbors, saying, 'Rejoice with me, for I have found the coin that I had lost.' Just so, I tell you, there is joy in the presence of the angels of God over one sinner who repents."

Or the experience of hope in 1 Peter 4:12–13: "Beloved, do not be surprised at the fiery ordeal that is taking place among you to test you, as though something strange were happening to you. But rejoice insofar as you are sharing Christ's sufferings, so that you may also be glad and shout for joy when his glory is revealed."

And the gladness in giving according to 2 Corinthians 8:1–2: "We want you to know, brothers and sisters, about the grace of God that has been granted to the churches of Macedonia; for during a severe ordeal of affliction, their abundant joy and their extreme poverty have overflowed in a wealth of generosity on their part."

In each case, the joy is experienced by individuals but bound up in its connection and celebration with a broader community by way of relief, of peace, and of community.[18] In this way, joy is proleptic, a foretaste, a way of being now that offers a glimpse of the way all things will be for all people. Joy is not a selfish, private experience but rather unites humanity at the nexus point between creation, God, and God's continued investment and involvement in creation. Delight, hope, and life appear where before they were not. Joy is bound up with gratitude, with an awareness of what could be versus what is, with defiance of what should not be while trusting that redemption and reconciliation are in the offing.

The late author and naturalist Paul Gruchow is compelled by the idea that even creation and the creatures within it can experience joy. He writes,

Birds, of course, do not sing for joy or chatter like hungry children, except, perhaps, in picture books for pre-schoolers. Let us say that joy is a cultural, not a biological, condition and that it is, therefore, improper to ascribe the emotion to a water ouzel. Even so, we would be right to say that our own reaction to the water ouzel . . . is capable of teaching us something about the nature of our own joy. Why, we might ask, does the water ouzel seem joyful to *us*? Never mind whether the bird itself is in fact joyful.

[John] Muir answers that the ouzel seems joyful because it sings in the face of adversity.[19]

It's precisely this absence of anxiety that courses through reflections on joy, religious and secular alike, across disciplines and perspectives. As I've often said on more than one occasion, Scripture offers up the imperative "Do not be afraid," but it thereby implies that there's something going on worthy of our fear! Modern systems studies encourage people toward a "self-differentiated non-anxious presence."[20]

People of faith might call this laudable nonanxious state a matter of trust, or of hope, or of peace. From a secular and psychological standpoint, Csikszentmihalyi has dubbed this experience "flow." When a person is not distracted by self-consciousness or worries but rather can concentrate on the task at hand, investing themselves fully in that moment, they experience flow, which

> often requires strenuous physical exertion, or highly disciplined mental activity. It does not happen without the application of skilled performance. Any lapse in concentration will erase it. And yet while it lasts consciousness works smoothly, action follows action seamlessly. In normal life, we keep interrupting what we do with doubts and questions. "Why am I doing this? Should I perhaps be doing something else?" Repeatedly we question the necessity of our actions and evaluate critically the reasons for carrying them out. But in flow there is no need to reflect, because the action carries us forward as if by magic.[21]

Csikszentmihalyi acknowledges that when one is in the "flow" of an activity, a key characteristic of that sensation is that the activity becomes "autotelic"—that is, defined less by the purported purpose and more by the action that is necessary to achieve it. For example, sports, played with the purpose of winning or gaining a scholarship, preclude the possibility of enjoying the sport for the sake of the sport.[22]

But while the experience of flow involves the Self, it need not be a selfish pursuit. In fact, what Csikszentmihalyi calls flow might, from a Christian perspective, be called a response to a vocational calling. A vocation, a calling from God, unites a person to a gift that is bestowed, nurtured, and encouraged by God and offered back not only to God but to the broader world. When that occurs, so does joy: life aligned with God, Self, and others.

Presbyterian theologian Frederick Buechner is famed not least of all for his quotations about vocation—namely, that "the place God calls you to is the place where your deep gladness and the world's deep hunger meet."[23] I've loved the sentiment and used it often enough (though I confess that the grammar fanatic in me winces at the dangling preposition). Still, a framework of joy would help round out the notion of "gladness" as it relates to vocation. Joy acknowledges that we are occasionally called to serve in ways that are unwelcome, harsh, and painful and that give reason for lament. But if we see our work as united to God's call, to God's community, and to God's promise, we can engage it with unified purpose, conviction, deep gladness, as Buechner says, and, even, thereby, joy.

Interestingly, in the Christian tradition, there is an apprehension about experiencing incarnate joy—joy of the *carne*, especially of the taste buds and of touch. But assumptions and pietistic traditions notwithstanding, Scripture is rife with divinely offered decadence to which all are welcome. Certain religiosities are averse to savoring the sensual, celebratory facets of life and love, but the late Lutheran theologian Paul Tillich was not among them. Tillich, I think, has some wisdom for us in these days. One of the ways he might offer us some fresh perspective about joy comes from an unexpected place, perhaps— his views about erotic love.

It's safe to say that eroticism is as close to a taboo word in Christian theology as any, but Tillich wanted to reframe and reclaim the notion of erotic love, and I think that his reasons why might help us rediscover beauty and joy in these days that otherwise seemed dimmed from either. To be clear from the start, Tillich understood *eros* to include the sexual but not to be restricted to that.

Instead, Tillich tries to highlight that a richer, more complete understanding of erotic love has to do with an appreciation of the inherent beauty, truth, or mystery of something or someone: "It strives for a union with that which is a bearer of values because of the values it embodies. This refers to the beauty we find in nature, to the beautiful and the true in culture, and to the mystical union with that which is the source of the beautiful and the true."[24]

As far as Tillich is concerned, then, you can have an erotic feeling directed toward a whole range of possibilities, including but not limited to "other humans, to ideas, to natural objects and those fashioned by human skill, to the divine source of all being." In fact, said Tillich, "without the eros toward truth, theology would not exist."[25]

In other words, best understood, erotic love pulls us into participation with that which is beautiful in an attempt to bond with it and to create more of it. Think, for example, of art. The creation of beautiful art and the appreciation of it inspire joy, contentment, and peace.

Think of the delight and thrill of a microbiologist studying a cell under a microscope.

Think of a scholar who has just discovered a new idea.

Think of a canoer floating on the still and quiet waters, settling in to hear the birds, see the moose, catch the fish.

Think of friends reconnecting over coffee or wine.

Each of these examples has to do with an understanding of the Self and an understanding of the Other, built on respect, curiosity, and a quest for the creatively beautiful, a desire to live not according to a figment of imagination or artificiality but with authenticity and connection. As Tillich writes, "Joy is possible only when we are driving towards things and persons because of what they are and not because of what we can get from them. . . . Mere pleasure, in yourselves and in all other beings, remains in the realm of illusion about reality. Joy is born out of union with reality itself."[26] And none of them have to do only with the Self; they are always the Self and another person or object of interest, beauty, and love. In a day and age when estrangement, retreat, suspicion, and disconnect are the modes of the day, erotic love invites something else: the appreciation, recognition, and joy of relationship.

In relief, though, erotic love also jars us into a recognition of the *lack* of relationship, of that which is *not* beautiful, or of the *absence* of beauty. In this way, Paul Tillich scholar Alexander Irwin says that erotic love poses a "threat" to systems of domination, of exploitation, of injustice. The more that we notice and are curious about the beauty and the integrity of the Other, the more we respect their integrity and worthiness. Our individual well-being is bound up in our communal well-being, and our communal well-being is bound up in our individual well-being.[27]

The unexpected (and awfully welcome) by-product is that by participating in erotic love toward the world, toward nature, and toward people—all different and distinct from one's Self, though some more than others—one can experience joy. (As a quick aside to all fellow introverts: Tillich's notion of erotic love doesn't mean that you have to be with a lot of people a lot of the time. It means that when you run into something Other, you see the divine there and treat the Other accordingly. Introvert to introvert, that includes, say, books.)

In Tillich's thought, explains Irwin, joy is "the manifestation of a healed connection to the created world and to the divine."[28] In fact, Tillich sees the opposite of joy not as pain but as detachment, as apathy, as simply not caring. Erotic love is exactly not that: rather than detachment, it is attachment; rather than apathy, it is investment; rather than not caring, it is compassion.

Certain people might see a theology of the cross lurking here: precisely where there is grief, there is the possibility of hope; precisely where there is abandonment, there is the possibility of connection; precisely where there is fear, there is comfort; precisely where there is ugliness, there is beauty to be rediscovered.

Erotic love, then, is protest love; it is engaged love; it is joyful love.

But in the spirit of calling a thing what it is, let's be clear: while erotic love can certainly be more broadly understood than it traditionally has been, eros is also very sexual. And believe it or not, there is the shockingly, sublimely, sensually, sexy, erotic even in Scripture, and we find it in the Song of Solomon, also known as the Song of Songs.

The Song of Songs is nothing, really, but a poem about extravagant lovemaking, male and female oral sex, yearning and searching and hiding and finding, all (quite shockingly, given the Christian bent toward sex only after a wedding has taken place) between two unmarried people, and moreover, one dark skinned and one light. Breasts are compared to fawns; a man's penis is described as sweet fruit and his scrotum as a bag of myrrh, the woman's genitalia as a garden of pomegranates that should be eaten; lips and mouths are honey and milk. Here is just a sampling:

> Your lips distill nectar, my bride;
>> honey and milk are under your tongue;
>> the scent of your garments is like the scent of Lebanon.
> A garden locked is my sister, my bride,
>> a garden locked, a fountain sealed.
> Your channel is an orchard of pomegranates

> with all choicest fruits,
>   henna with nard,
> nard and saffron, calamus and cinnamon,
>   with all trees of frankincense,
> myrrh and aloes,
>   with all chief spices—
> a garden fountain, a well of living water,
>   and flowing streams from Lebanon.

> Awake, O north wind,
>   and come, O south wind!
> Blow upon my garden
>   that its fragrance may be wafted abroad.
> Let my beloved come to his garden,
>   and eat its choicest fruits. (Song 4:11–16)

> I am my beloved's,
>   and his desire is for me.
> Come, my beloved,
>   let us go forth into the fields,
>   and lodge in the villages;
> let us go out early to the vineyards,
>   and see whether the vines have budded,
> whether the grape blossoms have opened
>   and the pomegranates are in bloom.
> There I will give you my love. (Song 7:10–12)

Never once have I preached on these texts from the pulpit, for obvious reasons. Preaching it is complicated for all sorts of obvious reasons, and even one not so obvious: God is never mentioned, not even by way of allusion, not even once, in the whole book.

Not once.

To make sense of how this positively erotic book found itself included in Scripture has moved many faithful believers, Jews and Christians alike, to use analogies to compare the passion of these two people to the love of God for God's people or to Christ's love for the church (which is particularly awkward, since the Song of Solomon was penned quite some time before Jesus appeared).

Most scholars, though, believe it to be just this: a gorgeous secular love song. The landscape itself is voluptuous and lusty and succulent; abundant and seductive love is commended; desire shows the woman to be the pursuer as well as the pursued; reciprocal affection is voiced; the creative and complete and unabashed giving of bodies is celebrated; and the unashamed expression of joy is in full bloom—all of which was believed, somewhere along the way, to reveal something of the sacred worthy enough to be included in Scripture.

There is such a thing as incarnate, carnal, biblical joy.

But other biblical examples of incarnate, carnal joy, sans sex, can be found laced throughout the Scriptures. New Testament theologian N. T. Wright points to any number of places in the Hebrew Scriptures that "reveal the robustly physical nature of joy." Dancing, singing, gifting, and good food and good drink are all marks of joy (2 Sam 6:18–19), not to mention the sharing of them with the wider peoples (Deut 14:29; 16:11, 14; 26:11).[29] Jesus was forever at parties in the Gospels. To name just a few examples, he turned water into wine (John 2:1–11); he was happy to eat at a banquet offered by a tax collector (Luke 5:27–39); he was called a glutton and a drunkard (Luke 7:33–35) and spoke of who should be welcomed at wedding banquets and ordinary table time at a sabbath meal (Luke 14).

We too can be so moved by an event that our bodies can't help but express joy in a different way—namely, by way of tears. For example, Allan Boesak writes—in the very first words of his book—that when Nelson Mandela was released or Barack Obama was elected,

> I am not ashamed to admit it: I cried tears of joy. Both times. We never dreamed that politics could look like this.
>
> Since 1994, two major and profound historical political changes took place that not only made and changed history but also created something within the human heart we had not experienced for far too long: a tidal wave of hope, not just for our politics but in our politics. That at the heart of it all should be black South Africans and black Americans, people who in so many ways bear in their bodies the scars of struggle for the sake of all humanity, and thus the bearers of so much hope for all humanity—"God's suffering servant for humanity," theologian James Cone calls them—made that hope more than just romanticized political hyperbole.[30]

It's a beautiful passage that twice refers to the manifestation of joy and its connection to hope: the tears Boesak wept when he saw Black men hold power and the wounds he saw their bodies bear—much like those of Jesus—scars that displayed both pain and yet, therefore, hope.

There is no way, of course, that all things will be as they should be this side of the New Creation. Complete joy will always be just that: a hope, never quite fulfilled, here always incomplete. But in the meantime, joy is a foretaste, in a sense, a dispositional trust that we are intended for joy. Perhaps joy is therefore all that sweeter because it is but a foretaste and also a reminder of that for which we were and are created. Therefore, where we do not see joy, we can be ambassadors of it and defy its counterexpressions by living all the more out of, into, and with joy.

I think more of us need to go to baseball games to be reminded of some humility and some humanity and of the interplay between loss and joy. I fell in love with baseball by way of the Minnesota Twins and by way of the first time I fell in love at all. In fact, given that I have absolutely no athletic ability whatsoever, it is not a far stretch to imagine that I fell in love with the Twins and baseball precisely *because* I fell in love. I don't know what else would have gotten me to the ballpark except for the promise of my hand being held by a boy who held my heart too.

Before this particular boy entered my world, I'd never entered a baseball stadium ever, except for the one at Carson Park in Eau Claire, Wisconsin, but that was just for the annual outdoor service held by the church where my father served as an associate pastor at the time.

I imagine that both loves were aided by the fact that at the time, in my mid- to late teens and early twenties, the Twins were on their late '80s / early '90s winning streaks, with the likes of Kent Hrbek and Kirby Puckett sending out the hits and bringing in the runs and the World Series titles.

It also didn't hurt that my high school love was Lutheran, and was handsome, and stole my heart the way Dan Gladden stole bases, and sent kisses my way as finely as Bert Blyleven pitched his ball straight across the plate, and was as dependable a presence in my young life as shortstop Greg Gagne was in all our lives, standing out on that field.

Truth be told, there isn't a single Twins game I watch without thinking of those days, days that are precisely what Van Morrison had in mind when he crafted what is perhaps the best summer love song ever, "Brown Eyed Girl." I knew joy in those games, and I remember it every time I sing that song as loud as my voice will let me.

My kids have gotten into the game and are now officially as fiendish about the Twins as I am. Else leans into those squeaker innings like I did when I was her age and still do.

But she is learning the lingo, and when Else doesn't know the rules, she looks them up to learn, and she wields that info like a pro while we are all munching our homemade Cracker Jacks, which we gnaw on every game when we aren't doing the same to our nails. She's my resident Twins announcer Dick Bremer.

And Karl, traumatic brain injury be damned, he knows when our guys are up to the plate, and he knows when to say that we need a home run (sometimes desperately), and thanks to our five years in Regensburg, Germany, he knows when the moment calls for a resounding *"Scheisse!,"* and though he can't jump up when we get a run like his sister and I do, he beams his grin, which is just as good as, if not better than, a celebration.

Part of the ambiance, the personality, of the game is its deliberate unrushed tempo. Baseball is less about a constant rush, is not about adrenaline fixes demanding regular top-offs, is no *Spaßgesellschaft* activity; instead, it is more about just showing up, about paying attention, and about being at the ready for the occasional thrill of those double plays, feeling the exhilaration of glorious line drives, and basking in the joy of the noble home runs.

That's not to say that fans *object* to a series of pell-mell cracks over the fence. While we all hope for those, much of baseball is not that. Much of baseball is an unglamorous *"e* for effort" at the plate, a slow pop fly hit or caught, a patient waiting for a batter to be walked, to be struck out, or maybe, just maybe, to hit that grounder that'll be so unexpected and fast, it'll be missed by the pitcher, who will inevitably reach for it, to no avail, and who will then turn to see the ball do everything short of wave as it passes on by.

Cue the obvious analogy to life: it's mostly about showing up and then expecting or hoping for a bit of lively drama injected into what is otherwise somewhat . . . routine. But that low-hanging-but-still-bittersweet-fruit truth aside, here's something else: true baseball fans, like the kind who buy their tickets and proudly wear their gear even in down periods, down seasons, and down decades, true baseball fans still show up.

We might groan at the pitches so far to the east that they land in Wisconsin, the dervish-like swings that miss all but the dust they stir up, the coulda-caught-it-with-your-eyes-closed dropped fly balls, but the fact is, no loss is ever just due to one person, and deep down, we know that. We might point to one Boy of Summer with one hand while smacking our forehead with the other, but still, we know that—generally speaking, at least—no game is ever entirely lost just because of one play or one player.

We don't say, for example, "Player X lost." We say "The Twins lost." In fact, we might even say "We lost," even if "we" weren't ever on the field. It's a collective loss, a collective "*Scheisse*." It's that "collective" responsibility—both for wins and for losses—that I find interesting.

Outside of the game, when some event brings about or notes Life, even the passing of it, we do so with a communal marking, and we throw open doors: joyful wedding receptions and birthday bashes and baby showers. Even funerals are most often held with other people who grieve or who care about those who are.

But when we drop the ball, so to speak, gosh do we tend to do that either in isolation or when we are left in isolation. Suddenly the collective interplay becomes the individual error.

Think divorces.

Think addictions.

Think arrests.

Think garden-variety poor choices.

On these sorts of occasions, it's awfully clear that "Player X struck out."

So who among us hasn't dropped a ball, hasn't swung and missed in a critical inning, hasn't committed an error of epic proportions? At least we're out there, one could say. So sure, we all strike out, sometimes quite gloriously. And yet if you're not a real-life baseball player, if you are just like the rest of us mere mortals, never putting foot to field but only swinging foot out of bed, you, we, are often left to our losses alone, because our actions, or lack thereof, in down periods, down seasons, down decades, are deemed undeserving of patience, support, or public allegiance. What's most remembered are our really bad plays.

And sometimes we fear that we aren't even remembered at all, least of all by God.

That's messed up.

———

I'm not the first one nor will I be the last to notice that going to a baseball game is like going to church. We may believe in different teams/congregations/denominations, but we all go to worship just the same. We've been going to the cathedrals for years and years, and we'll keep going for years and years to come. Outfits change, rules even change, but the love of the game and the crowd and the Cracker Jacks doesn't.

Baseball even has saints, those who are the best that baseball offers up, and while we might all hope to be one someday, most of us just stand in wonder and awe before them, inspired by their stories, encouraged that maybe, just maybe, we could be sort of like them one day, and in the ordinary (and reality-grounded) meantime, we are simply reminded of the incarnate beauty of the best of the game that we get to see in living, breathing motion.

In some ways, you see, baseball is what church, what a believer, aspires to be.

You struck out? Go on, sit down, spit some chew, swear away from the cameras, and then come on up to bat again in a spell.

Maybe you'll do better. Maybe you won't. But you're still welcome on the plate again, regardless, again and again.

Getting tired on that mound of yours? Well done, good and faithful servant. You go take a rest now. Someone else has got it from here on out.

You sick and tired and hurt? You seem like a good candidate for the injured list. Sit down; we'll help you heal, and meanwhile, others have it covered.

You committed an error for all to see? I ask you, Who hasn't? So, yeah, we're mad. But we've got your back. We'll come back. We'll cheer you on again because although we know that your stats won't ever shake that blunder, your stats are more than that blunder too.

———

Every season, I worry that the Twins are going to break my heart like that first boy did years ago—and like most everyone since then, come to think of it. But if they do, I will forgive them.

I'll be back. And so will they.

And who else do I need, anyway?

I have my son, I have my daughter, I have my father, and I now have David, whose hand I now get to hold, and who, albeit not yet a baseball fan, at least isn't cheering for the Yankees, the Chicago White Sox, or the Brewers. I have my three hounds, I have gratitude and grins that far outweigh any regret and remorse about the loss of those sweet young-love-and-young-life days, I have Van Morrison, and I have tickets to see the Twins at least once per season.

It is enough.

At the end of the day, perhaps joy is in the satisfied, grateful, content, hint-of-more-to-come "In this moment, it is enough."

3

Finding Hope When You're Losing Your Grip

"Don't worry, be happy." You just need to hear those four words, and the tune made famous by Bobby McFerrin begins to hum itself.

But earwormy song or no, and with all due respect to Mr. McFerrin, we all know that sometimes there *are* worrisome things, and sometimes we *do* have reason to be sad. In fact, the World Health Organization states that over 264 million people are depressed—a distinctly different circumstance than sadness but with some corresponding experience. Mood disorders caused by depression and stress are a leading cause of disability across the globe. The National Alliance on Mental Illness (NAMI) states that in the United States alone, depression affects 19.4 million people (7.8 percent of the population) and that those diagnosed with depression have a 40 percent higher chance of suffering additional health issues, from cardiovascular to metabolic diseases, than the rest of the population. An increased risk for personal isolation, job loss, and even suicide naturally corresponds with these statistics.[1]

We are becoming aware, though, that our individual and communal response to depression has and too often still is not adequate because acknowledging the reality of mental health issues is often, albeit increasingly less so, a taboo topic. The abiding stigma surrounding mental health unfortunately connects internal struggles with weakness, fragility, questionable emotional stability, and therefore questionable dependability. People don't tend to acknowledge—sometimes even to themselves—feelings of emotional instability or wellness. Even garden-variety experiences of sadness, anger, or fear go unmentioned and therefore go unnoticed.

After withdrawing from several Olympic events, Simone Biles took hefty dings for her heroic decision. She was dubbed a "quitter," an "embarrassment," and "selfish." But she also racked up praises, not least of all for leading the way—along with other athletes like Michael Phelps and Naomi Osaka—to more open conversations about mental well-being. Teens and young adults, precisely the age of most Olympians, are also the demographic in which mental health issues begin to surface. The athletes' willingness to acknowledge their own struggles provided permission for a wide swath of people to do the same—Google statistics indicate that after Simone Biles withdrew, searches related to mental health hit a two-month peak.[2]

It isn't an illusion that emotions often deemed to be "negative" are hard to shake. Of course, people seek to avoid pain, emotional or otherwise, and even more so when the unwelcome feelings linger. Once they've made a home in one's spirits, these emotions can seem to be permanent. Studies demonstrate that sadness affects people for a longer time than other unwelcome emotions, such as fear or anger. Fear, for example, lasts an average of half an hour, and sadness persists for almost five days.[3] Repressing the acknowledgment of sadness can, in fact, lead to depression; this pattern is what feminist scholar Soraya Chemaly calls "self-silencing." This tendency seems to afflict girls most, this habit of filtering one's negative feelings due to embarrassment, uncertainty, or lack of trust. Prior to puberty, depression is diagnosed equally across gender lines, but between twelve and fifteen years old, girls triple in their rates of depression and, not coincidentally, are diagnosed with anxiety and other mood disorders at a far higher rate than boys.[4]

So when asked, "Are you OK?" we say, "Absolutely!" When we start to catch our eyes welling or even drifting into some unseen horizon as we contemplate something that causes us grief, we might even literally shake our heads to shake off the feeling and try to move on with our day. But it turns out that feeling our negative emotions and claiming them personally or even out loud might be the very thing that will usher in well-being again. Martin Luther has struck it right again: calling a thing what it is yields hope.

For example and surprisingly, studies are suggesting that those who endure sadness are better positioned to respond to life's stresses in more adept ways than those who aren't. Australian social psychologist Joseph Forgas has discovered that people who identify as sad demonstrate "better judgment and memory, and were more motivated, more sensitive to social norms, and more generous" than those who were happy. Sad people more aptly discerned the dynamics of a situation, were more motivated to make both personal and systemic changes based on their perceptions, and were also better able to extend compassion and generosity to others.[5]

It might seem counterintuitive, but Forgas and his collaborators propose that sad people have more of a vested interest in reading the room and in reading themselves so that they can move through and beyond the reasons for their melancholy. Consequently, sad people tend to be more attentive to and retentive of the cues, vibes, and information at hand and suspicious of their first reads, wanting to ensure that they have absorbed all the available input before trusting their perceptions or, for that matter, the perceptions of others.

Similar truths seem to apply to the most shunned emotion: anger. Turning again to Chemaly's *Rage Becomes Her*, she urges that anger not be ignored, tamped down, or rejected but rather welcomed and embraced as an indication that something wrong is afoot. Anger is a barometer, of sorts, one that indicates when a shift has occurred or an indicator that notes when there's a gap between what is and what should be. Chemaly defines anger practically with a poetic lilt. Of it, she says,

> Anger is an assertion of rights and worth. It is communication, equality, and knowledge. It is intimacy, acceptance, fearlessness, embodiment, revolt, and reconciliation. Anger is memory and rage. It is rational thought and irrational pain. Anger is freedom, independence, expansiveness, and entitlement. It is justice, passion, clarity, and motivation. Anger is instrumental, thoughtful, complicated, and resolved. In anger, whether you like it or not, there is truth.
>
> Anger is the demand of accountability. It is evaluation, judgment, and refutation. It is reflective, visionary, and participatory. It's a speech act, a social statement, an intention, and a purpose. It's a risk and a threat. A confirmation and a wish. It is both powerlessness and power, palliative and a provocation. In anger, you will find both ferocity and comfort, vulnerability and hurt. Anger is the expression of hope.[6]

This take on anger is not exactly first-pass characterizations of it. Typically, anger is associated with rage, with being unhinged, with reactivity. There is a reason for this, of course: anger is hardly a pretty emotion to feel or to see. But Chemaly senses the same thing that Walter Brueggemann does—namely, that the suppression of anger, not least of all by way of lament, ultimately creates the potential for an unhealthy explosion of rage: precisely what is generally associated with the feeling of anger. But it's the suppression of anger rather than the healthy expression of it that gives rise to dangerous manifestations of anger.

To put a spin on a Shakespearean line, the truth of anger will out: the question is whether it will be released in a healthy or in a toxic, dangerous way, even harming the person repressing it. When a person feels anger, they release both adrenaline and cortisol, hormones that arise in moments of stress. These hormones are useful, even from a basic evolutionary perspective. If you are in a moment of threat, danger, or indignation, both cortisol and adrenaline aid quick thinking, quick action, and, if necessary, quick fleeing. But over the course of time, too much cortisol or too much adrenaline can harm our bodies. Raised cortisol levels increase glucose levels, reduce the body's capacity to fend off disease and other ailments, and contribute to weight gain, osteoporosis, mood swings, and increased thirst and urination. Too much adrenaline increases blood pressure, heart rate, and the probability for heart attacks, headaches, strokes, and a general unpleasant demeanor. Just normal adulting can cause abnormal production of cortisol and adrenaline, but when there is the addition of cultural, political, and personal stresses, those levels can rise even further.

Ordinary stresses, says Chemaly, are a form of threat. While our *minds* can distinguish between a tiger, which we don't run into on an average day, and a chronically tight schedule, or an empty bank account, or a frayed relationship, our *bodies* can't distinguish the difference, and so they suffer the physical effects of being poised for alert. Covid has made us more on the alert, more stressed, and more vulnerable to its ill effects. Women, as it turns out, are more vulnerable to the negative health effects of stress, not least of all by way of repressed anger, because they are culturally vulnerable to the expectation that they suppress their anger. In short doses, that is, stress can save your life, but over the long haul, it can do you in.

Chronic caregiving, work claims, relationship challenges, persisting grief, constant conflict, and even just normal adulting cause stress. Life can be a hurricane, and it's sometimes hard to find or stay in the eye, the calm in the midst of the storm.

Once, I had two good friends, conveniently also therapists, who came over once every other week or so for wine. Both have a habit of meditating, of just sitting.

"Sitting?" I say. "That's all you do? You sit? Tell me of this sitting thing of which you speak."

A while back, I told a Spent Dandelion retreater this tale, and she sent me a clip from an episode of *Star Trek: The Next Generation* showing Counselor Troy, her mother, and Worf's son enjoying a bubble bath. And then it pans to a deeply annoyed and confounded Worf: "So," he seethes, "you just sit here?"

That's me. I'm Worf. It's not that I'm opposed to sitting. It's that my life is opposed to having me sit! Albeit for different reasons, I think that we all crave more times to just sit. The thing of it is, when I'm sitting, I'm never just . . . sitting. I'm writing, consulting, taking care of bills, on the phone, and so on.

Turns out that the word *anxiety* comes from the Latin *anxietatem*, meaning "anguished, troubled," and is directly related to the word *anger*, which comes from the Latin *angere*, which means, quite literally, "to torment, to tighten, to squeeze," and to the English word *anguish*, which comes from *angustia*, meaning "a choking sensation, distress, or even rage." Interestingly, the word *eager*, often confused with the word *anxious*, has a similar word history, coming from the Old French *aigre*, which came from the Vulgar Latin *acrus*, both meaning "harsh, bitter, sour, acidic, sharp." And if you think you are noticing some similar English words, you are right: *vinegar*, which comes from the French words *vin aigre*, or bitter acrid wine, means "sharp and unpleasant to the taste."

Anxiety has a cousin in stress. It wasn't until the 1950s, says immunologist Esther Sternberg, that the term *stress* was coined by a physiologist named Hans Selye. That was because precisely at that time, technologies started to come into their own in his field, offering the ability to measure physiological responses. Dr. Selye realized that when the body was stressed, the hormonal and blood pressures manifested just like pressure in the world of engineering and physics. So he adapted and adopted the word *stress* from these fields into his own. In fact, Sternberg notes that he went around the globe trying to get that word—that very word—into the languages of every dictionary across the world. I heard Dr. Sternberg interviewed on the podcast *On Being*. (If you haven't heard of this show, hosted by Krista Tippett, forget everything else I say and listen to it right now.) On the podcast,[7] Dr. Sternberg even mentioned the Germans who talk about being *gestresst* and that something is very *stressig*! And it's true!

But it didn't take the term to be coined for people to notice and study its effects. In the 1880s, says Dr. Sternberg, it was observed that there were five causes of "modern" stress: "the periodical press, the telegraph, the steam railroads, the sciences, and . . . the mental activity of women."

Right.

But as Dr. Sternberg notes, what was really being described was the effects of the Industrial Revolution. And she says this:

> Now, but why is it these things are stressful? Because change, novelty, is one of the most potent triggers of the stress response. And that's a good thing because when an animal finds itself in a new environment—so if a field mouse wanders into a new field, if it didn't have a stress response, if it wouldn't suddenly sit up and look around and become vigilant and focused and ready to fight or flee, if it just went to sleep, it would get eaten by the next cat that came along. Right?
>
> So, you need your stress response to survive. And novelty must, therefore, trigger the stress response. So, the problem

happens when the stress response goes on too long, when it's active when it shouldn't be active, when you're pumping out these hormones and nerve chemicals at max. And that's when you get sick, and that's when these chemicals and hormones have an effect on the immune system and change its ability to fight disease.

So change is stressful, and therefore it can even cause illness, disease, and other related toxic consequences. And because that isn't enough, studies, Dr. Sternberg goes on to say—and her assertions are corroborated by all sorts of research I've done in the areas of psychology and neurology—that when children are exposed to constant stress (neglect, abuse, anxious environments), their brains change.

They do.

They fundamentally get wired differently, and it doesn't just happen to children. Instances of trauma, of violence, of long-term fatigue and long-term abuse in adults have been shown to create new brain wirings and structures.

After Karl's brain injury, I learned that brains need time to heal. Some of you who may have had or know of people who have had strokes know of what I speak. Not only do brain injuries need healing, but people with brain injuries tire more quickly, they get overwhelmed faster, and they crave quiet more. I have described Karl's brain injury to some people by using the state of South Dakota, which, as you may know, looks pretty much like an 8½ × 11 sheet of paper.

So in the lower right-hand corner sits Sioux Falls, where we lived for some time. In the lower left-hand corner is Rapid City. The fastest way to get from Sioux Falls to Rapid City is to hightail it on Interstate 90, which is essentially a straight line between the two. But if I-90 is rubble, if it is under construction, then you need a new route. But it's clearly a detour. Ideally, then, you'd hope to coast just south or north of I-90. Trouble is, that road is wrecked too. So you need to take, in effect, a detour from the detours. The upshot is, to get to Rapid City, you need to buzz to Watertown in the upper right-hand corner, then to Aberdeen smack-dab in the top center, then to Huron in the center of the right-hand third of the page, then to Brookings squarely in the middle on the right edge, then up to Buffalo in the upper left-hand corner, then to Pierre absolutely in the middle of the paper, then to Winner in the bottom middle of the page, and then finally to Rapid City.

That's how it is with a wounded, a healing, a tired brain. Neural pathways that were once there, or were once well-traveled, are not.

They are in repair.

They might never be repaired. These detours might become the main route. And it's possible that they can even become quick routes over time. But the point is, when your brain is injured by way of physical or mental trauma, it takes longer to do tasks that would otherwise be easy.

Darby Kathleen Ray, associate professor of religious studies and director of the Faith and Work Initiative at Millsaps College in Jackson, Mississippi, writes eloquently about the need to rest:

> To live deeply requires rest and reflection. Occasional binges of inactivity or vacation—mere crisis management—will not suffice. . . . Sabbath time is time out of the rat race; time spent not on producing, consuming, or desiring more but on cherishing what we already have—time spent deepening relationships and cultivating no market values such as gratitude, mercy, mutuality, humility, and joy. Above all, sabbath time is rest, intentional and deep. . . . Contrary to Market time, sabbath time is not outcome oriented. It is not linear, teleological, or recognizably productive. Rather, it meanders, lingers, and spirals. Sabbath time dilly dallies, as my mother would say. . . .

When the nourishing rest of sabbath time becomes the foundation for our work in the world, that work holds new promise. It is not that the daily grind disappears or that systems of injustice are suddenly transformed. The desire for work that is personally meaningful, socially valued, and adequately compensated remains unfulfilled for most people, which means the struggle to rethink work and its defining systems must go on. And yet, despite these sad realities, rested work—work as it is viewed from the standpoint of rest, and work that is nourished by deep rest—gestures in significant ways toward transformation.[8]

So how is it that we find comfort in the chaos, that we find the time to sit, or meander, or Sabbath, when the only thing that spirals, it seems, is life . . . our congregation . . . our country out of control? How is it that the encouragement in Psalm 46:10— "Be still, and know that I am God"—is felt as a balm for rather than salt in the wound? We are finite, and there is not one thing that we can do about it. We are finite; we can't save the world alone; we can't save our nation, the church, our congregation, our families, or ourselves. We are finite, and alone we can't stop the slander, stop the liturgical seasons, stop the presses. We are bound and we are bounded. There is innate frustration within that truth, but there is also innate grace: we cannot do it all.

We can't.

So after the relief of that obvious-but-overlooked truth settles in and settles us down, more questions come:

1. What is it that we can do?
2. How do we tend to ourselves to both do what needs to be done and cope with the loss and frustration of what we can't do?
3. How is it that we can tend to others who are parched, and dry, and brittle?

At hand is the need for restoration, a term that at its root comes from the same word as "restaurant." Who knew? In fact, the French soup maker who came up with the word *restaurant*, a Monsieur Boulanger, sold soup at his shop that was so good, he promised that it would "restore" the spirits of all who slurped it down. He was so convinced of it that he had a conflated Latin version of Matthew 11:28—"Come to me, all who labor, and I will give you rest"—inscribed above his store's window, the word *rest* being, in Latin, *restaurabo*.

For People of the Banquet, I think we can work with that. To be restored is to be fed.

We are hungry.

Hungry for rest, hungry for calm, hungry for justice, hungry for kindness, hungry for grace, hungry for, just once, no laundry, no dishes, no bills due.

We are called to feed and yet yearn to be fed, to be restored, to come to the Restaurant, a place with space and willingness given to create, to be re-created, to recreate.

Restoration can be done in isolation, but at the same time, it can't be done in isolation. That is, we need others to give us the opportunity, not to mention support, for restoration. For example, I find no small amount of self-satisfied glee that when I'm off to present a speech or a seminar, it takes about seven people to cover what I normally do all by myself. I also experience no small amount of deep gratitude that the people in this entourage of support lend their time, their efforts, and themselves to my family's aid.

A restaurant restores because there are people who need to be restored and there are restauranteurs. That is, a Communion of the Saints is here in part to be the community of restoration, of restorers. Leaning into attentiveness to others' needs, acknowledging our own needs, admitting that balm is needed and then having balm ready to be offered, this is the communion of saints and the reign of God at work and in motion, so that when *we* need to rest, we don't have to work and be in motion.

Given that stress and isolation contribute to mental unwellness, perhaps one form of that grace might be the extension of practical forms of help: not just thoughts and prayers but rather, say, comfort, rest, meals, childcare, laundry folding, errand running. Banal proverbs like "God never gives you more than you can handle" or "Just trust Jesus!" or "Give it all to God!" are harmful and insulting when someone is overwhelmed by stress or grief. But providing tangible, active salvation (*soteria* in the Greek, literally meaning "health, healing, and wholeness") is a different matter entirely. Such help relieves causes of stress and implications of it.

Dr. Suzanne Simard, a forest ecologist, has done extensive work to demonstrate that trees actually communicate with one another, nurturing, protecting, and literally standing in solidarity. It's been dubbed the "wood wide web," which is both kitschy and catchy. Her discoveries are astonishing, as is she, and left alone at the ecological level, we could marvel at them, and it would be enough. But Dr. Simard thinks this pattern of boreal communication and mutual support serves as both a model and a mirror for humanity.

Ten years ago, Dr. Simard got breast cancer. Through it all, she kept thinking of what she learned about and from this forest ecosystem. The community of women to which she now belonged, collectively fighting breast cancer, connected with one another to give support, information, and presence. "It's like the [tree] network, right?" she says. "It's a reinforcing, resilient network. It's regenerative. It helps you be happy and healthy. And you know, in the forest, that's how forests regenerate . . . how seedlings establish within the network of this collaborative system; you know, the old trees, they're nurturing them and bringing them up. And this is exactly how our own social systems work and what keeps us healthy and alive and productive and happy, too."[9]

Dr. Simard knows that death is part of the life cycle, but she says that we are built for resilience and regeneration. The strongest may survive, but *only* because of their interconnection with others. When you combine interconnection and reciprocity with the rest of the community (and here's the kicker), the whole community becomes strong.

A "survival of the fittest" model has deeply informed capitalism, American foreign policy, the US spirit, and even denominational structures. These latter structures remain keenly interested in how much money is being brought in and how many members are on the rolls, as every rostered leader who fills and sends off the annual report knows and as if either of those is a marker of fidelity to the gospel.

But Dr. Simard's research poses contrary theories, like were we to value interdependence rather than independence, we would be communally healthier and individually stronger. Were we to nurture one another, particularly in times of stress and depletion, perhaps we could once again see, love, marvel, and have the breath to feel joy at the vast, global, real, and metaphorical forest for all the deeply interconnected, thriving, real, and metaphorical trees.[10]

The North American love affair with independent grit, though, creates a context of shame to admit that one needs help and a subtle measure of judgment for those who do need help. On top of that, communal applause is raised for people who survive by their own mettle—as if they did. But Dr. Michael Unger, social scientist and researcher in the field of reliance, rebukes those tendencies: "Self-help fails because the stresses that put our lives in jeopardy in the first place remain in the world around us even after we've taken the 'cures.' The fact is that people who can find the resources they require for success in their environments are far more likely to succeed than individuals with positive thoughts and the latest power poses."[11] Self-help might treat the symptom, but perpetual self-help is self-depleting. We can't do life alone.

But alone is what we might feel when overwhelmed. And those of us who have fewer "resources required for success" feel the weight of isolation. What we call resilience is often masked privilege and entitlement.

It seems to me that congregations and individual Christians, however, are perfectly suited to provide the sorts of resources Unger is describing. "Today salvation has come to this house," said Jesus in Luke 19:9, when Zacchaeus joined him at the table, gave away his own possessions, and promised to repent of fraud. Multiple times we hear variations of the phrase "Your faith has saved you" (πίστις σου σέσωκέν σε), as in Luke 7:50 (the forgiveness of sins), Luke 8:48 (healed hemorrhage), Luke 17:19 (the healing of leprosy), and Luke 18:42 (healing of blindness). The healing that Jesus provided happened in that immediate moment and provided respite, rejuvenation, and renewed hope. What are Christians and Christian communities if not ambassadors of the salvation of Jesus?

Andrea Mazzarino, social worker and cofounder of Brown University's Costs of War Project, realizes that suggesting that "living a privileged life in the United States while learning about violence in faraway places constitutes 'trauma' will seem understandably laughable to many. Yet . . . if you're empathizing with others to the extent that you should be, there is a remarkably small psychological difference (at least in the moment) between bearing witness and experiencing an event yourself."[12] Perhaps those who offer *soteria*—care, support, or help in the name of Jesus—*are* martyrs of sorts, are *witnesses*, taking on the pain so that another's pain burden is lightened. It's another version of the Nguni Bantu word *ubuntu*, often translated as "I am because you are." A word more familiar to many might be *compassion*, which literally means "to suffer with" someone. Be it by bearing witness to someone else's pain or reason to hope, by living according to the spirit of *ubuntu*, or with compassion for another, we cannot be understood, let alone survive, without one another.

The trees, Dr. Simard would tell us, have known this all along.

Dr. Resmaa Menakem a "cultural trauma navigator," psychotherapist, and a social commentator, draws attention to a nerve, of all things, that can pick up another's emotional state as well as reveal to us our very own. It's the vagal nerve, and it is the transmitter of what is often called the "gut instinct." That's no coincidence, as it travels to and through the gut. Menakem has done extensive research on this nerve, and he believes it to be one reason why we can sense, even when far away from someone beloved, how another person is doing.

The nerve itself is known by any number of names: the vagal nerve, as above, or the vagus nerve, or the wandering nerve, or, as Menakem likes to call it, the soul nerve. It runs from the brain through the face, the chest, the stomach, and down to the abdomen, making a pass through the liver, spleen, pancreas, and both intestines. While it does connect to your brain, it only does so via the brain stem, what Menakem calls your "lizard brain," because it is the fight, flight, or freeze center of your response system.[13] So it's a threat-perception nerve. When you feel an emotion, particularly one related to a stressful feeling, such as anger, fear, anxiety, or grief, your voice becomes taut, you feel a lump in your throat, your breathing increases, your body clenches, your stomach tightens, and your bowels may open. That's all thanks to the vagus nerve. In contrast, when you are relaxed, your soul nerve "knows" that and sends a message throughout your body that it is safe to breathe deeply, loosen your muscles, and take in the peace.[14] Those who have suffered epileptic seizures may have a vagal nerve stimulator inserted just below the collar bone, as has my son postinjury. The stimulator sends regular electrical impulses through the nerve into the brain and thereby shocks the brain into normal patterns.

In short, Menakem says, our soul nerve informs us physically of what we are feeling emotionally and what others are feeling as well. It thereby opens us to vulnerability, this scary nexus of pain and joy: pain at the loss we feel at the suffering we encounter and joy mingled with relief when it is seen, heard, met by someone else. It's an emotional place that is often avoided, for the assumption is that vulnerability puts us in a position of weakness and risk—which, to be fair, has shades of truth to it. But Brené Brown flips this around, saying that vulnerability is really the avenue to courage: "Feeling vulnerable, imperfect, and afraid is human. It's when we lose our capacity to hold space for these struggles that we become dangerous."[15] The antithesis, arguably, to vulnerability is invincibility.

All of us are vulnerable, at the root. None of us are invincible. Moreover, to be invincible takes a lot of work. The compulsion to be vulnerable comes from expectations of perfection and from fear that one can't make the perfection cut. But when, in contrast, a culture allows space for mistakes, room to be wrong, and permission to fail and thereby learn, people's motivations shift. Studies indicate that in *this* sort of environment, productivity and creativity both increase along with a sense of satisfaction and pleasure in one's task at hand.[16]

In a culture that expects perfection and disdains weakness, it takes some skills to learn how to tamp down anxiety. Menakem calls such techniques "settling." It's a way of engaging the external stress that can't, itself, be reduced. The practice of settling opens the spirit to come to terms with one's mistakes, one's trauma, one's finitude, and it extends energy to that process rather than to the pursuit of pretending that none of that is true. To be settled, says Menakem, means to be open to engaging the healing that needs to happen.

Mindfulness, a term often used in these contexts, sometimes conveys the idea that we are to let the pain wash away from us, to give it up, to let it go. Menakem, however, is wary when techniques associated with the quieting of the spirit provide an escape from it instead. He writes, "Instead of inviting and accepting healing, [these contrary techniques] use settling in a neurotic way, to avoid healing. When they face a conflict or difficulty, they don't settle themselves and then work through the clean pain. Instead, they flee the situation, and then partly soothe and settle their bodies with meditation, prayer, yoga, hiking, and so on. They use settling as a form of dirty pain, rather than as support for moving through clean pain."[17]

Clearly, he has no grudge against meditation, prayer, yoga, or hiking. His concern rises rather when these techniques are used to avoid confrontation with the pain. Facing the trauma acknowledges it and taps one's own strength to move through the trauma and even beyond it.

Exactly along these lines, Rabbi Danya Ruttenberg offers an intriguing exegesis on the traumatic story of Abraham and his willingness to sacrifice first Hagar and Ishmael to the wilderness and then his son Isaac to God. In the first story, Sarah commanded Abraham to banish Hagar and Ishmael, God backed her up, and Abraham did so with textual silence, "even," says Rabbi Ruttenberg, "to tell his own son goodbye." Next, God requested that Abraham kill Isaac by way of a burnt offering. Again, Abraham consents to the request with no objection.

Ruttenberg is perplexed by his acquiescence because Abraham has already boldly challenged God about Sodom's fate. But regarding his own sons? He's mute. How could this be? Ruttenberg poses an interesting thought, one rooted in the Jewish midrash (teaching) on the book of Genesis, compiled in a text called Genesis Rabbah 38, written somewhere between 300 and 500 CE. In it, a story is told of how Abraham's father pitched him into a furnace as a punishment for Abraham smashing the idols his father sold.[18] The midrash describes a childhood in which Abraham was himself abused and abandoned by his father, left to die. Rabbi Ruttenberg maintains that Abraham had no model that could provide a different way of being for his sons,[19] and so the cycle not just of abuse but of unsettled pain continued.

Trauma endures in part because closure can be tremendously difficult to experience. You may wish that you had had the wit, the patience, the mental and emotional presence to refute and reject the source of pain: a hold-your-own comeback, a physical resistance, the courage to leave. Menakem believes that, even if symbolically, the completion of the traumatic arc is key to healing. Any number of options are available to do so: engage the affronter, if not risky; envision an engagement with the affronter; resolve within yourself what should have been done or said or practice what you would say the next time; if an unwelcome next time *does* come to pass, learn from and trust yourself to let the future play out differently than the past.[20]

Confronting past trauma—and engaging the lament that rises from it—causes pain, but a different sort of pain than the initial wound: it's pain that heals rather than inflicts. And it is a pain that is metabolized with intentionality. The pain of trauma can be avoided but never ignored. It thereby festers and ultimately demands far more energy—spiritual, emotional, mental, and physical—than does directly addressing it.

Refusing to acknowledge pain or seeking to reconcile it continues to give the trauma power and permission to define you. "Calling a thing what it is" provides an avenue to relinquish *pain* rather than the possibility of joy again.

Again, we are led to the notion that joy is the transformation of pain.

It is relief from trauma and the experience of life in contrast to loss.

It is the triumph of vulnerability and the consequence of courage.

It is the release of anxiety and the knowledge of shalom—hard-won peace.

When this process has been allowed to be completed, says Menakem, the body can "settle." The body and the spirit are allowed to relax, to breathe, to experience contentment and safety. And he makes the case that this sort of healing can happen not just in individual bodies but in the communal body too. Regarding white supremacy, for example, he says that "accepting clean pain will allow white Americans to confront their long-time collective disassociation and silence. It will enable African Americans to confront their internalization of defectiveness and self-hate."[21]

White people know, in a visceral sense, that they have much to lose if the system of white supremacy is lost: a righting of wrongs insists that the pattern of wrongs be righted, and this means pain to those in power. To avoid "settling" into, for example, the pain of the loss of privilege, Menakem says that the collective white amygdala becomes engaged, that rudimentary part of our brain that responds with one of three options: fight, flight, or freeze. Unfortunately, our processing mind is the last to kick into gear when a threat is perceived. He writes, "That's why when we put a hand on a hot frying pan, the hand jerks away instantly, while our thinking [brain] goes, *What the hell just happened? OW! THAT SHIT IS HOT!* It's also why you might have the impulse to throw the pan across the kitchen even though doing so won't help you."[22]

Buddhist teacher of meditation Sharon Salzberg has noticed that people have discovered several ways to allow them to skirt what needs to be faced, to avoid clean pain and the settling that is necessary to experience it. The first, she says, is to cling to a person, a circumstance, the very pattern that in fact needs to be changed. Attachment, as the Buddhist tradition would call it, is a refusal to allow a thing, a person, a Self to change.

A second adverse coping mechanism would be anger or fear of change or a fear of the "other": she calls it aversion, as in an aversion to metabolizing the truth that a shift in one's reality or status quo is coming or needs to come. Anger manifests itself, she says, in an outward flow of energy and fear in an inward one, but both seek to "declare it untrue"—namely, that something new is occurring, or soon will.[23]

Another way of responding to a challenging new thing is to sleep. I feel seen here. When I am overwhelmed, a nap never sounded so good: it's a miniescape that needs only a ticket to the couch and thirty minutes of time. Conversely, one can become unfocused, fretful, distracted, restless, as Salzberg calls it. Neither option—fatigue nor hyperactivity—provides the focus to attend to a task or an emotion or a situation that needs one's full presence.

Last, she says, is the act of doubt. Doubt, she says, is often one's ally: it provides necessary skepticism to give room for asking key questions, to not just evaluate but reevaluate options, to challenge the motivations for one's choices. However, when doubt becomes cynicism, one has no impetus to invest time into the project and may even latently despair that something new could ever come about.[24]

I imagine most of us can appreciate each of these methods, healthy or not, of coping with stress. Dr. Sternberg compares the experience of stress to the experience of being lost in a maze: you turn, and each way offers either a certain dead end or an uncertain corner. Heart rates increase, anxiety spreads through one's core, desperation begins to seep into every moment.

But what would happen, she asks, if we could shift the paradigm and envision ourselves less in a maze and more, instead, in a labyrinth? A labyrinth, a patterned path on a floor, has no false dead ends but rather invites a person into a process, meant to be taken with intentionality and gentle pace, with a beginning and an end, and with opportunities for reflection, observation, and forward movement.[25]

The grounding that a place provides, as with a labyrinth, is a source of tremendous healing. When my children and I arrived along the North Shore of Minnesota, we were leaving somewhat chaotic years in South Dakota. We knew that being here among the trees, the hills, and Lake Superior, all of which were literally outside our door, gave us peace in a way we hadn't anticipated and, frankly, we didn't know we needed.

About a week after we arrived, the clouds turned dark and the winds picked up in ways that for us, coming from the prairie, were all too familiar. Our instincts immediately went to protection from a tornado, which meant heading to the basement. While we have a basement in our home, unlike in our former house in South Dakota, we had no lift to help my son access it. So we called the one neighbor we knew to see how concerned we needed to be about life-threatening storms here. She laughed. "Oh, no one can remember the last time that we had a tornado here. The Lake just sucks the storm's energy right on up."

It's become a perfect metaphor for the effect that this place has on stress, not only for our family, but on those who visit our retreat center. There is something about this place, a sacrality of space, that absorbs our stress, or reframes it, or gives us breath to tackle it.

The pandemic, though, complicated matters. People were not able to get out, at least not safely, precisely at the time that stress was on the increase rather than the decline. In an article in the *New York Times*, psychologist Dr. Adam Grant observes that at the pandemic's beginning, our personal and communal amygdalae were on fire, eager to protect ourselves and our loved ones, to keep death and sickness at bay. And yet as days turned to weeks turned to months turned to years, routines replaced the frenzy, and then . . . there was stasis. Very little changed in procedures or possibilities for getting out, and we had to adapt to a lack of community and a lack of focus. All of this led to a banal feeling of blah. Grant writes, "It wasn't burnout—we still had energy. It wasn't depression—we didn't feel hopeless. We just felt somewhat joyless and aimless. Certainly, the angst of the last several years of political life and pandemic life have lent themselves to a feeling that could arguably be best expressed as 'meh.' It's a lukewarm, distracted state of being, one that is characterized by a lack of focus, of zip, of energy. It turns out there's a name for that: languishing."[26]

In the same article, Grant also refers to Csikszentmihalyi's concept of flow, when one feels utterly unified with one's Self, one's environment, and the task at hand. Nothing else matters but the synchronicity of the moment. People who did—or to be more precise, could—immerse themselves in their work, despite the pandemic's chaos, avoided languishing, enjoyed more satisfaction with life, and may have even experienced happiness despite the bane of Covid.

Typically, he says, and even ideally, flow can be experienced when you are "in the groove" of a project, a conversation, or an athletic act. But even being able to engage in a hobby, a book, a puzzle can engage one's mind in a way that keeps it active and challenged.

It's a remedy to the fractured way of thinking that has plagued so many during the pandemic. Studies, Grant says, indicate that only a small sliver of people can focus with other claims on their attention. "Computers," he writes, "may be made for parallel processing, but humans are better off serial processing."[27]

When distractions are the norm, a lack of progress is too. This inability to accomplish a task is deadening to morale, not to mention professional reputation and personal self-respect.

Having opportunities to experience, to quite literally en-Joy a feeling of flow, he says, is the "most important factor in daily joy and motivation." Flow is, in a real sense, a deep connection to one's Self and to one's environment. Again, Csikszentmihalyi's theory resembles the Lutheran notion of vocation. Ideally, one's vocation treasures a dynamic relationship between one's internal sense of Self, as shaped and supported by God, and one's external context, which is also shaped and supported by God. Each has a need for and can be blessed by the other.

When the flow between them is interrupted, each vocational partner, so to speak, suffers in distinct ways. The larger environment misses out on the full contribution of the individual who is otherwise distracted, while the individual feels alienated not just from one's broader community but even from oneself: if you are thwarted from doing what you are called to do and to be, you are thwarted from being fully you. You are alienated from both your role and your Self.

For this reason, from the perspective of Dr. Teresa M. Amabile and Mr. Steven J. Kramer, writing in the *Harvard Business Review*, people should "treat uninterrupted blocks of time as treasures to guard. It clears out constant distractions and gives us the freedom to focus."[28] More to the point, it also gives us freedom to be who we are called to be: dedicated time to engage our callings honors our communities and honors both what we are called to be and the One who has called us to that pursuit.

Relatedly, flow can describe the synchronicity between not just ourselves and our environment but ourselves and our past and our future. Buddhism offers some helpful ways of making the point. It refers to *dukkah*, or the experience of stress, anxiety, and resistance to our reality, and *sukkah*, or an existence that is not necessarily carefree but has developed the capacity to let go, to release, that which cannot be changed.

Dukkah comes in both physical and mental expressions; one response to *dukkah* events is to try to control the situation or the source of our suffering. The results often do not go well. The futility generated by our inability to calm our anxiety only causes, in turn, more anxiety.

Sukkah, in contrast, meets struggle with a sense of peace and calm, a confidence that even in the midst of challenges and uncertainty, our moment and our mood are determined not by reactivity but by a steadfastness and confidence that transcends the chaos of the moment.

The origins of both terms are rooted in Sanskrit and an Aryan nomadic group who traveled by way of cart. The word *dukkah* meant having a bad axle, and *sukkah* meant driving with a good axle. Douglas Abrams describes this concept in *The Book of Joy*: "Not a bad metaphor for life."[29] And it isn't: when one resists reality, the road traversed is bumpy. When we acknowledge our reasons for anger, distress, and dis-ease, we conserve stress and anxiety, and we can instead harness it to accept and cope with what is rather than what we wish would be. As Abrams says, "So many of the causes of suffering come from our reacting to the people, places, things, and circumstances in our lives, rather than accepting them. When we react, we stay locked in judgment and criticism, anxiety and despair, even denial and addiction. It is impossible to experience joy when we are stuck this way. Acceptance is the sword that cuts through all of this resistance, allowing us to relax, to see clearly, and to respond appropriately."[30]

It's akin to the notion that the amount of pain in one's life is directly related to the distance between one's reality and one's expectations. The greater the distance between the two of them, the greater the dismay. Both poles, of course, can be shifted: one's expectations can be lowered to meet reality, and albeit with more effort, one's reality can be altered to more closely meet one's expectations.

The question, of course, is, By what metric do we gauge our reality and our expectations? As Csikszentmihalyi noted, Aristotle claimed that nothing was more important to the enterprise of being human than a pursuit of happiness. Any other attainment is perhaps valuable in and of itself but necessarily because we expect it will provide us happiness—more money, more status, more influence. He continues,

> Despite the fact that we are now healthier and grow to be older, despite the fact that even the least affluent among us are surrounded by material luxuries undreamed of even a few decades ago (there were few bathrooms in the palace of the Sun King, chairs were rare even in the richest medieval houses, and no Roman emperor could turn on a TV set when he was bored), and regardless of all the stupendous scientific knowledge we can summon at will, people often end up feeling that their lives have been wasted, that instead of being filled with happiness their years were spent in anxiety and boredom.[31]

Something beyond an attainable thing must be able to provide us with joy. In this way, Csikszentmihalyi retells of how, in his poem *Prussian Nights*, Aleksandr Solzhenitsyn found some solace in the midst of an agonizing imprisonment by the Soviets for his critiques of Stalin. Solzhenitsyn found that he was able to feel as if he were above and away from the crisis of the moment, escaping the horror by being transported by his thoughts of poetry.[32] Likewise, Csikszentmihalyi wonders whether (to return to the importance of place and joy) perhaps the place is not only a physical one but also a spiritual one. Transcendence takes place in what is often called a thin place. It's an uncertain, nebulous, vulnerable space. There we aren't sure of where we are or, depending on our circumstances, whether we are: all are open, including possibilities.

In *The Necessity of Empty Places*, Gruchow retells his travels across several states to spend time in the sorts of spots people drive through or around or fly over. Gruchow writes, "Every important religious prophet has spent a sojourn in the wilderness and has found there some source of strength important to subsequent belief. What is this source? It is, I would suppose, the product of having successfully faced danger and deprivation, of having, in Kierkegaard's phrase, overcome the world: It is joy."[33]

I think Gruchow nailed it.

Joy is the source of hope and resilience despite, and to spite, death.

In turn, hope and resilience despite, and to spite, death is the source of joy.

Now to find the ways to avail oneself of both.

4

Justified for Joy

———

Lutherans go big on the idea of a vocation. The word is rooted in the Latin word *vocatio*, which means "calling." It's different from a "job." A job is something that you *have* to do and can range from a chore that has to be crossed off a list to work that has to pay the bills. A vocation, though, is a calling, something you can't *help* but do because God has summoned you to do it.

Luther spoke of it this way: "Thus every person surely has a calling. While attending to it he serves God. A king serves God when he is at pains to look after and govern his people. So does the mother of a household when she tends her baby, the father of a household when he gains a livelihood by working, and a pupil when he applies himself diligently to his studies. . . . Therefore it is great wisdom when a human being does what God commands and earnestly devotes himself to his vocation without taking into consideration what others are doing."[1]

Note that everything Luther lists here is related to both an individual's identity and the community's need for it. So relatedly, when Lutherans talk about vocations, which we are wont to do, we make mention of an inner call and an outer call: we feel stirred to engage in something—a career, advocacy, a relationship, a decision—and that stirring is affirmed by others. If one or the other of these is missing—that is, if we feel called but others are unenthusiastic or if others present an option to us and we feel uncompelled to take it—then either a job or a choice to be avoided is at hand, but certainly a vocation is not.

Typically, however, the idea of a vocation, a calling, is brought up in the context of work: someone is called to be a pastor, called to be a homemaker, called to be a builder. You see it in the list of vocations mentioned by Luther himself. There is something tangible that is produced by living into and out of one's vocation.

But I can't help but wonder what would happen if we were to consider self-care as, itself, a vocation. I am convinced that care for our "selves" is as worthy, and as foundational, as the care of others and the care of creation.

I joke that R.E.M. is only a band to me. Because of my son's TBI, I sleep next to him to help and protect him at night. For example, when most people snooze, they will effortlessly turn or stretch their legs in the night. But Karl's like a beetle on his back; he can try to move, but mostly he just wriggles. So I'm there to slide my feet under his to pull them straight or to lift him up to flip him—in a good and gentle way, of course, rather than like a pancake on a griddle.

Sometimes Karl has episodes of myoclonus, which *look* like a seizure but aren't. They're simply full-body involuntary muscle spasms. Hiccups are a form of myoclonus, but Karl's myoclonus is like getting hiccups on steroids. His whole body, right down to his eye muscles, is wracked by violent twitching.

I have so many questions for God.

Between helping him stretch, helping him turn, attending to tremors in the night, and the occasional coyote howl, bear visit, or wandering skunk that catches the attention of the two dogs who sleep on my bed, I don't sleep well at all. It's not so much that I have given myself permission to take naps: I can't help *but* take naps. I used to feel guilty and terribly sheepish about it. My Apple Watch wasn't helpful as I sought to give myself nap absolutions.

My Apple Watch takes it upon itself to announce, randomly throughout the day, that it's determined, "It's time to stand now!" Every time it does, I glare at it. I am a single mama. I am self-employed. I get no sleep.

Psalm 127:2 pretty much simultaneously describes and explains a lot in my world, and it adds some level of existential dread:

> *It is in vain that you rise up early*
> *and go late to rest,*
> *eating the bread of anxious toil;*
> *for he gives sleep to his beloved.*

Sometimes I've wondered whether God and my Apple Watch are in cahoots. There should be some setting, maybe even a default one, on the stupid thing for single, self-employed mamas who get no sleep. If *I* were to design an Apple Watch, I'd make one that would say, depending on the time of day and life circumstances, "It's time to nap now!" or "You should have a glass of wine now" or "You should have both a glass of wine and a nap now."

These would be far more relevant to my life.

I understand the point of the reminder: standing on occasion to break up habits of sitting all of the time is healthy. It is definitively *not* healthy to sit, and sit, and sit. But I do think that I'm not alone in hunching that we might be on the move more than we give ourselves credit for or than we even should. We might be more frenetic than we realize. We might need a nap more than we need a stand.

I have come to think that we use activities, be they work or hobbies, as a way of justifying ourselves and proving ourselves to others . . . and perhaps most of all to ourselves. The busier our lives, the more we seem to think that we can make the case that we're not sloths (with all due respect to sloths). Sometimes, life is busy, and you don't get enough sleep, and that is just the way it is, right? Like, *you* go and tell the coyotes in the middle of the night to keep it down.

Life sometimes intervenes like coyotes in the night.

Deadlines loom, shifts need to be clocked, bills need to be paid, laundry piles up, and friends want to meet. But all of that being true, here is what is also true: perhaps a guilt-free nap, a canceled nonessential event, a nap, a declined invite, a nap, maybe a mental health day, with a nap, perhaps these things need not be sources of apology or sheepishness. Instead, perhaps they can be moments where we recognize that we are not finite.

We are limited, not least of all by what we can do, by how much we can do, and by when we can do it. Perhaps intentionally taken pauses are occasions when we can consider a dose of humility. In *Lighten Our Darkness: Toward an Indigenous Theology of the Cross*, Douglas John Hall writes this: "The discovery of limits can only be for us the most traumatic experience. Our entire continental experiment has been based on the mirage of limitless horizons. Limitless land, limitless resources, limitless opportunities, limitless human know-how, limitless freedom. So thoroughly has the spirit of uncircumscribed potential been absorbed into our North American consciousness that to begin to question it is almost an outrage. Of all the aspects of the optimism that has informed our way of life, perhaps the most unshakeable is the belief in limitlessness."[2]

So many things here catch my attention but perhaps most especially the word *traumatic*. That's a kicker. It's *traumatic*, Hall says, to realize that we are finite. So we stave off that realization by filling up our schedule with endless commitments and plans and people.

Infinite people don't sit.

They stand.

And they fill up circles that show steps and heart rates and exercise bands. Moreover, they can even share their "success" with others for encouragement (and maybe even a gloat?). Ironically, I'm quite sure that in our attempt to stave off the traumatic, we cause ourselves trauma.

In Exodus 3:5, God told Moses to take off his sandals: "Then [God] said, 'Come no closer! Remove the sandals from your feet, for the place on which you are standing is holy ground.'"

Anathea Portier-Young, associate professor at Duke University, points out that sandals were worn for journeys, for protecting oneself against rough paths, and as a symbolized status—or lack thereof. But, she goes on to say, when "Moses removes his sandals he will find himself at journey's end, at the true goal of every journey. He will release himself from every claim so that he can accept the claim God makes upon him. He will strip away strivings for status, success, and stability. He will find his true ground and he will know where he stands."[3]

He will know where he stands.

Maybe, then, that's the thing for the Apple Watch to consider, for us to consider—we don't need a "Time to stand" reminder. We need a "Know where you stand" reminder. A "Take off your shoes and take a load off while you think about it" reminder.

Maybe we need a "This place is holy ground" reminder—and a reminder that this exchange with Moses and God took place on ordinary ground made holy because God was there. Because God is everywhere, perhaps right this very moment, any number of us should take off our shoes. We could sit while thinking about where we stand. We might turn off our phones, close our eyes, and take a nap to give us a refreshed perspective to consider where we should stand when we get up, for we are worthy of rest, of care for ourselves, of restoration, and of self-love.

Scripture is filled, of course, with references to love, but often they concern the love for or of another. Most famous, at least at weddings, is a passage found in 1 Corinthians 13:4–7: "Love is patient; love is kind; love is not envious or boastful or arrogant or rude. It does not insist on its own way; it is not irritable or resentful; it does not rejoice in wrongdoing, but rejoices in the truth. It bears all things, believes all things, hopes all things, endures all things."

The word rendered "love" here is the Greek word *agape*. It's referring not to romantic love (that's *eros*) but to benevolent love, even self-sacrificial love. Paul's describing here a love that is, of course, to be hoped for in a marriage but isn't exclusive to it either. Instead, Paul is addressing the sort of love that is to be shared within Christian community—for one another and for the world.

That notion of sacrificial love, however, can mess people up, especially, historically, women. It's lent itself to the notion that relationships demand a person's essence to keep their partner content.

But nope.

Recall another text, this one found in Mark 12:28–34:

One of the scribes came near and heard them disputing with one another, and seeing that he answered them well, he asked him, "Which commandment is the first of all?" Jesus answered, "The first is, 'Hear, O Israel: the Lord our God, the Lord is one; you shall love the Lord your God with all your heart, and with all your soul, and with all your mind, and with all your strength.' The second is this, 'You shall love your neighbor as yourself.' There is no other commandment greater than these." Then the scribe said to him, "You are right, Teacher; you have truly said that 'he is one, and besides him there is no other'; and 'to love him with all the heart, and with all the understanding, and with all the strength,' and 'to love one's neighbor as oneself,'—this is much more important than all whole burnt offerings and sacrifices." When Jesus saw that he answered wisely, he said to him, "You are not far from the kingdom of God." After that no one dared to ask him any question.

This passage, especially verses 31 and 33, has long caught my eye, not least of all from a feminist perspective. It's fairly clear from the text and its reference to Deuteronomy 6:5 that the takeaway is that we are not to live selfishly. Instead of giving *ourselves* the benefit as we are wont to do, we are to see ourselves in the Other and treat them accordingly. There's even a wonderful parallel saying the followers of Pythagoras had: "What is a friend? Another I."[4]

But hidden in the call to love one's neighbor as one loves oneself is the imperative, the implicit expectation, that we are also to *love ourselves*.

If we have no Self left, we cannot offer it for the sake of another.[5] In fact, Valerie Saiving Goldstein, a female graduate student in theology in 1960, laid the groundwork for rethinking the idea that the source of all sin is pride. Goldstein says fine, that works if you're a man, but the purported *antidote* to it, humility, is what we women do too much of anyway. *Humility*, she said, is the source of *feminine* sin, evidenced not least of all in the sacrificing of the Self for the sake of the Other so that there is no longer any Self to give.

Every night, I bless my children twice: First, I ask, "Are you comfy? Are you cozy? Are you content? Do you know that you are loved? Because that is the *most important thing*." Second, I say the child's name followed by "You are *beautiful*. You are *safe*. And *I love you*." And then I make the sign of the cross on their foreheads and say, "And *so does God*."

I want them to know that when—not *if*—their hearts are for any reason broken, when they feel alone, when they *are* alone, that they are nonetheless loved and lovable. I want them to know that they are treasured beyond someone's potentially capricious or selfish external word or action. They are, within and in and of themselves, beautiful and beloved.

What has happened in them, however, is more than I could have expected when I started this blessing ritual well over a decade ago. They have learned that when they suffer mild disappointments to adult-sized hurts, they can withstand the loss. They have learned that knowing that they are loved by their mother and their grandfather and dear friends and family with whom we share our regular lives, they are willing and able to engage the world despite the real possibility that it might reject them, or hurt them, or be flat-out scary. They have learned that while their sense of lovableness cannot be dependent on ultimately untrustworthy external people or forces, their knowledge of self-love, which comes from deep mama love and deep God love, is *fiercely* dependable.

They have learned that there is no point in comparing themselves to others, people who may portray a vision of themselves that does not jibe with their reality. In an interview with Krista Tippett, Brené Brown herself confesses how she got caught up in this tendency to hold oneself up to another person's apparent accomplishments and gifts and, in fact, to try to be them. People who have this tendency live such frustratingly unattainable lives, which, of course, doesn't stop them from striving to have the impossible: "nail polish [that] doesn't chip, no stretch marks, no struggles . . ."[6] Brown simply noticed how easy it is to keep getting caught in the attempt to have what others have, to be what others are, and to do whatever it takes to have and be that.

But there are costs to this endeavor, she goes on to say, no higher than the costs to our own well-being. There is, she says, external and internal shame in engaging in self-care, such as resting, playing, relaxing, engaging in hobbies. We fear that these sorts of means of self-love are not only perceived as necessary only for the weak and lazy but also counter to our need to justify ourselves on the basis of how much and what we produce.

Our self-care is sabotaged by our society's care about stuff and status and wealth. Cornel West defines our society, in fact, as "decadent." He writes that society "suffers from what Arthur Miller called the disease of unrelatedness, where people quest for relations and intimacy and suffer a lack of community and solidarity. It's just a spiritually impoverished way of being in the world. . . . Nonmarket values of love and care and service and laughter and joy run counter to that seriousness of maximizing personal preferences and maximizing profits. It's just a very impoverished way of being human, you see."[7]

Personal well-being matters, but not at the expense of communal well-being. And personal well-being ought not to be defined by the materialistic values treasured and extolled by capitalism, the communal metric of North American life, one that misconstrues materialistic success as the source of joy.

It takes intense energy to resist the values and virtues of a commodified existence. A well of wellness, of faith, of community, and of communal support is key, which helps sustain a stance of being in the world, even embracing it, being shaped by it, and yet not ultimately defined by it. It's not a relaxed stance, as West knows, and in fact, he says that this posture, this way of engagement, involves "combative spirituality." That language is intense, drawing up imagery of battle, of conflict, of cortisol! But West envisions a position of empowerment. You must combat the powers that be, forces that are antithetical to a Christian way of being. Surprisingly, he says, in these moments and living in this way, faithful followers of Jesus experience, of all things, "subversive joy," which draws upon and manifests "the ability to transform tears into laughter, a laughter that allows one to acknowledge just how difficult the journey is, but also to acknowledge one's own sense of humanity and folly and humor in the midst of this very serious struggle. It's a joy that allows one both a space, a distance from the absurd, but also empowers one to engage in the struggle again when the time is necessary."[8]

Call it an edginess, the James Dean approach to Christian faith, the community of rebels with a cause: there is a joy one receives from living life with authenticity, aligned with powers that seed life and that refuse to cede power to its nemesis. There is joy in the freedom of this promise: now that we know that death doesn't win, there is more to do with our lives than preserve them. Savoring and spreading delight instead of death may take energy, but it gives it right on back by way of individual and communal joy.

This joy is not the stuff of platitudes, positive thinking will not bring it about, it is not a panacea, and it cannot be created or sold or bought. Instead, it's an essence defined by the knowledge that God has been, is, and will be present in our pain to bring about peace.

I find it fascinating that in English, the word *know* covers at least two, if not three, kinds of knowledge. We know that it is cold outside, and we know our friends. The first use, however, is informational knowledge, and the second is relational knowledge. But other languages distinguish between the two. In German, for example, the verb *kennen* refers to knowing some*one* (*Ich kenne dich*, or "I know you"), and *wissen* refers to knowing some*thing* (*Ich weiss, dass es mir kalt ist*, or "I know that I'm cold"). French and Spanish too use a different verb for each sort of knowing: *connaître* and *conocer* and *savoir* and *saber*, respectively.

There is, though, yet a different form of knowledge: that of wisdom. In Hebrew, the word for this sort of knowing is often referred to with a wink-wink and a nudge-nudge as "knowing someone in the biblical sense." The word, though, is *yada*. Some rumors suggest that George Lucas used this word as inspiration for Yoda's name, for it means a fullness of knowledge or wisdom.

I've come to wonder whether wisdom, *yada*, is the middle, overlapping portion in a Venn diagram of relational knowledge, informational knowledge, and experience. I wonder if it might not also be at the nexus of joy. We know one another, we know of God's transformational history, and we know of our life's griefs and hopes, and with this confluence of knowledge, we are all the wiser for it.

The Western world has defined joy by the metrics of produced success, accumulated goods, and marketable possessions, but the joy of creating and participating in play, delight, and art has not been valued as "productive," and in fact, it has been treated with disdain, as indulgent. Cornel West, though, sees these activities precisely as ways to defeat and even transform oppression and despair and as signs of that transformation. He need point no further than Toni Morrison's *Beloved*. In the novel, Baby Suggs welcomes people to the hidden safety of forested sanctuary space. She says to the Black community that had followed her and gathered into that space,

> Here in this here place, we flesh; flesh that weeps, laughs; flesh that dances on bare feet in grass. Love it. Love it hard. Yonder they do not love your flesh. They despise it. They don't love your eyes; they'd just as soon pick them out. No more do they love the skin on your back. Yonder they flay it. And O my people they do not love your hands. Those they only use, tie, bind, chop off and leave empty. Love your hands! Love them. Raise them up and kiss them. Touch others with them, pat them together, stroke them on your face cause they don't love that either. You got to love it, you! And no, they ain't in love with your mouth. Yonder, out there, they will see it broken and break it again. What you say out of it they will not heed. What you scream

from it they do not hear, What you put into it to nourish your body they will snatch away and give you leavins instead. No, they don't love your mouth. You got to love it. This is flesh I'm talking about here. Flesh that needs to be loved. Flesh that needs to rest and to dance; backs that need support; shoulders that need arms, strong arms I'm telling you. And O my people, out yonder, hear me, they do not love your neck unnoosed and straight. So love your neck; put a hand on it, grace it, stroke it and hold it up. And all your inside parts that they'd just as soon slop for hogs, you got to love them. The dark, dark liver—love it, love it, and the beat and beating heart, love that too. More than eyes or feet. More than lungs that have yet to draw free air. More than your life-holding womb and your life-giving private parts, hear me now, love your heart. For this is the prize.[9]

Love your body, love your heart, love them alone, love them together, for they are worthy of love, and they are holy, even when, precisely when, the world would have you believe that they are not. We are all worthy of love, and that includes not just loving our body but loving the good things of creation and inviting others into it.

The late theologian Walter Bouman and his wife, Jan, loved this world and were committed to making this world a better place. They did so in many ways. For example, they had a bedroom in their basement, and when it was empty, they opened it to someone without a home, believing it made no sense to have people with no beds and beds with no people.

They lived on his salary, a modest income for a seminary professor, and they gave hers away, a modest income of a public school teacher. While teachers never make enough, their gifts made a healthy enough deduction on their taxes that they got audited regularly. The Boumans gave money to the seminary, to the church, to the Democrats, to public radio, to Bread for the World, and to whoever else they thought served the reign of God.

Students would line up at the Boumans' door at around 4:00 ("It's 5:00 somewhere," he always said somewhat defensively) to be served nuts and martinis or manhattans. The Boumans would purchase four tickets for a string of days at the Stratford Festival in Stratford, Canada, and then gift two of the tickets to another two people—and even provide a place for them to stay for the duration.

And every year, Walt and Jan also bought a block of four season tickets to the Columbus Symphony. Each concert night, they invited a different couple to join them for the show and for dinner at a five-star joint in town, the now gone, then exquisite Handke's Cuisine. The fine wine, fine food, and fine music were all on them. It was because the evening was a matter of stewardship too.

Jan and Walt firmly believed that providing a bed to the homeless and money to organizations bent on serving others demonstrated the reign of God. So does friendship fostered over gourmet cuisine and gourmet music, because they believed that God delights in good things and delights in us enjoying good things too.

As best as I can and when I could, I've tried to emulate Walt and Jan: inviting people to a good meal and for good music. I've discovered that people are always a bit uncomfortable with someone else picking up the tab. People are usually uncomfortable with grace, I've decided.

But discomfort aside, in the days when I lived in a city rather than the woods, we'd enjoy together a feast and laughter and raw stories and a brisk walk to the concert hall and then enthrallment with the musicians who somehow always transported us away, and then we'd return home, albeit a bit changed.

Those evenings of good food and good conversation and good music tend to do that: they transport us to another place and leave us transformed just a bit and somehow unable to help but steward the experience beyond the night.

Experiencing nights like that makes one declare "That was very good" and want to bring forth a bit more goodness . . . not because one has to but because one can't help but radiate forth what one has encountered by surprise and by grace.

Joy, it turns out, is rooted in God and the goodness of God's creation and the contagious celebration of them. It's sacramental, even. Despite a tradition of people coming forward with somber faces to partake of the Eucharist, it's intended to be a joyous feast: we are all invited to the Lord's table! This is for you and is given for all people to be strengthened but also to en-Joy!

Hedonism is not the new gospel, of course. Instead, Douglas Abrams reflects on the late Archbishop Desmond Tutu's perspective on joy as it relates to peace. Abrams learned that joy can reframe peace—or perhaps even more apt, shalom—for us: "Being more joyful is not just about having more fun. We're talking about a more empathic, more empowered, even more spiritual state of mind that is totally engaged with the world. When the Archbishop and I were working on creating a training course for peace ambassadors and activists who go into conflict regions, he explained how peace must come from within. We cannot bring peace if we do not have inner peace. Similarly, we cannot hope to make the world a better, happier place if we do not also aspire for this in our own lives."[10]

Yet our own lives intersect with others, not least of all by way of the Sabbath. Perhaps there is no better way to gift ourselves with self-care than by finding time not just for rest but for communal sabbath and joy, for coming together to remind ourselves that we are not no-body but are part of a body, that of Christ.

We are bound together—the root of the word *religion* means "to bind together"—in a common claim that death does not win.

Perhaps in addition to the holy habits of helping, like supporting food pantries, homeless shelters, and community gardens—things the church tends to do anyway—it might be worth exploring how, as a fundamental part of Christian ministry, churches can empower individual selves to encourage self-care and thereby self-love.

How do single mothers find rest?

How do chronic caregivers find time to breathe?

How do the poor find ways of paying bills?

How do transgendered people seeking clarity find it and celebrate themselves?

How do the disabled find community?

How do those who are taxed for time, for space, for security, and for peace find sabbath?

Or what would happen if fancy stewardship season kickoff suppers were abandoned forevermore (inveiglement of the worst sort) and replaced with decadent dinners just because?

Lack of rest, lack of breath, lack of wealth, lack of clarity, lack of community, lack of sabbath, lack of celebration: each of these and more is an obstacle to joy. But for those who yearn for such experiences *and finally do experience them*, they are the very *sources* of joy. And insofar as this is true, congregations and individual Christians can, in the name of Jesus who brought *soteria*, be ambassadors of a proleptic offering of God's joy.

This said, a key and perhaps paradoxical counterpoint is this: many churches have "joy" in their congregational names, and had I been on the selection board for any one of them, let alone been asked, I would have advocated with all my might against the idea. At the very least, I would have fought to include mention of *pain*, or *grief*, or at the very least *hope*—any word that at least acknowledges that not all is well—in the congregational identity. "The Community of Lament and Joy," say.

When one has been struck by pain, to belong to a congregation that only has "joy" in its name leaves one wondering, Is my grief welcome here? Can I acknowledge my anger? Is it safe to say that I am not always happy? What happens if I am too tired to think of coming to church, let alone to be joyful?

If I sit in these pews, am I allowed to lament?

But *that* said, if congregations see themselves as ambassadors of joy, perhaps they might see the people who ask these questions differently—they might even, for the first time, *see* these people.

Perhaps congregations can, through the lens of joy, detect where it is missing and then can impart it, bestow it, gift it, embody it.

Perhaps they can offer people tangible means to self-care because all selves are worthy of love and worthy of the blessing of, the experience of, the delight of, the relief of, the promise of joy.

5

Holy Saturday Living

In his *Free of Charge: Giving and Forgiving in a Culture Stripped of Grace*, theologian Miroslav Volf retells a marvelous story of Ernest Hemingway, found in his short story "The Capital of the World": "Madrid is full of boys named Paco, which is diminutive of the name Francisco, and there is a Madrid joke about a father who came to Madrid and inserted an advertisement in the personal columns of El Liberal which said: PACO MEET ME AT HOTEL MONTANA NOON TUESDAY ALL IS FORGIVEN PAPA and how a squadron of Guardia Civil had to be called out to disperse the eight hundred young men who answered the advertisement."[1] It's a gorgeous story and one that gets to the anxious yearning we all have to be forgiven, to receive grace, and our hopefulness that we, even we, will receive it.

Our entire culture is an *if/then* culture: If you mow the lawn, then you get ice cream. If you finish your homework, then you may play. If you wear the right clothes, then you will be accepted. If you work, then you get health insurance. If you are white, then you won't get shot at a traffic stop. If you are thin and rich, then your life will be glorious.

But grace operates on a whole different metric.

Grace operates on a because/therefore model.

Because you are my child and it is hot out, therefore you get ice cream. Because homework can be a bear, therefore you should take a break and play. Because you are being fully who you are, therefore you will be welcomed as you are. Because you are human, therefore you deserve access to care. Because you are valuable, therefore your life is worthy of defense no matter what. Because your body is made *imago Dei*, therefore you are beautiful. Because you are a child of God, therefore, no matter what, you are worthy of grace, you are forgiven, you are loved.

There's a story, perhaps apocryphal, about Roy Harrisville during a debate in the 1960s about whether women should be ordained. As the back-and-forth died down, he stood up. The room was silent. "Of course," he bellowed, "women do not deserve to be ordained." The crowd was stunned. After an appropriate rhetorical pause, he said, "Neither do men."

Grace is evidenced precisely because you have not earned what you are about to get.

If you earned what you are getting, it would be a reward; it's compensation, it's karma, as some parlance would describe it. But if it is grace, what you are receiving is not because of what you did and who you are but exactly in spite of the same.

Joy is a bit like grace.

Joy is the experience of delight, of relief, of contentment known most of all when you know full well that an alternative experience is available. Joy is the experience of joyful defiance and finding and reveling in hope where there is none to be had.

———

To be clear, hope and I have had a dicey relationship. On the one hand, whether we realize it or not, just swinging our legs out of bed is a hope-filled move. Hope, even subconscious hope, allows us to function. We hope that we will have a good day, that we'll get to work on time, that our loved ones will get home safely; we marry, we have children, we move, we retire. All are trajectories of hope.

But sometimes hopes are dashed. Quite literally, actually. Mine were dashed across a street.

Since then, I hope for Karl's complete healing from his brain injury, and everything I do is geared toward making that hope tangibly true. The reality of that occurring is slim. And so then what good is hope?

So I have come to wonder about the toxicity of hope. Can hope itself be detrimental? Can it thwart one's acceptance of reality? Does it allow one to live a quixotic life built on vanities and illusions?

Yep.

But the danger of succumbing to hope's opposite, despair, is equally numbing.

And I don't particularly like the blandness of mere optimism either. When Karl is sick, I am optimistic that his fever will go down. But I hope he will walk around the corner and tell me that he's feeling fine again.

So I have made peace with hope in the same manner as I engaged my first pregnancy, a pregnancy that ended in a miscarriage. I had been told that many first pregnancies end in miscarriages, almost as if my body needed to learn what to do. And when I did miscarry, I grieved, but I did not despair, and we did not give up and were blessed with Karl and later Else.

I refuse to give up on the possibility that Karl can heal. And I insist upon going to great lengths to make the impossible possible. My vocation as a mother calls me to that pursuit. And vis-à-vis God, it gives me an opportunity to remind God of God's promises. I do so in a hold-God-accountable-to-God's-promises sort of way. It is manifestly evident in Scripture that God's agenda is healing. Perhaps it's the Jew in me who feels quite comfortable pointing that out to God.

After the accident, when the doctors (bless them, bless them, bless them, heroes all) told me that all indications were that Karl would never walk again, I gulped. Would he talk again? "*Nein!*" they said. Would he ever make his gorgeous mischief again? "*Nein!*" they said.

To each "*Nein!*" I replied, with every fiber of my being, "*Doch!*"

Doch is a multipurpose German word, a word that, depending upon how many times it is said and with what amount of vehemence, is either an intensifier or a corrective. To illustrate, someone from Florida who visits northern Minnesota in the spring, when the thermometer has incrementally risen to fifty-two degrees, might hear a local say, "It's warm!" to which the Floridian would reply, "*Doch!*" But come late fall, were they to hear a Minnesotan say, "I can't wait until all the snow comes!" the Southerner might reply, "*Doch, Doch, Doch!*"

Now, years later, albeit with great help and not on the regular, Karl *can* walk. And he can definitely with a thickness of speech *talk*. And there's no question that he makes all *sorts* of mischief again. So Karl and I now have a shtick. I ask him, "Karlchen, when the doctors said that you would never talk again, or walk again, or laugh again, or make mischief again, what did I say to them?" And he says with a smile and with every fiber of his being, "*Doch!*"

Doch equals spoken hope.

Doch is defiance in the face of death.

Doch is a moving-toward-Easter word.

Doch is a Holy Saturday word.

Doch is a word that understands the reality of death but makes choices despite it—and it is based on something other than it.

And suddenly I can wrap my mind around hope against hope.

Our family has thrown our lot into a life of *Doch*; we acknowledge that death is real but refuse to cede to death another win. The word is even on our license plate for Karl's conversion van. (That one friend of mine pulled me aside in the grocery store and asked why and how I got *douche* on my plates is beside the point.)

James Cone says that when Black Christians gather at church, they were and are reminded that "trouble and sorrow would not determine our final meaning."[2]

They knew the Spirit of Joy and the Spirit of *Doch*.

Doch is German. But Greek offers us *prolepsis*, another word of defiant hope and joy.

Prolepsis means a taking beforehand—it is the Greek version of the Latin word from which we get our word *anticipate*, which means the very same thing. To live life proleptically, to live life in anticipation of the reign of God, means that we live life as if the reign of God were fully here now.

But prolepsis is not only a future-leaning word; it is also a past-leaning word, because proleptic thinking values memory. We know something of the future promises because we know something of past pains, past joys, past teachings—found in Scripture, creeds, liturgy, rituals both communal and personal—and past promises of who we are called to be. C. S. Lewis wrote of his childhood in his memoir *Surprised by Joy*, and in it, he noted that joy involves both memory and longing: "All joy reminds. It is never a possession, always a desire for something longer ago or further away or still 'about to be.'"[3] Mary Clark Moschella refers to this passage and draws Lewis's thoughts out: "The experience of joy is something intensely felt, perceived as an ancient memory bubbling up from deep inside even while it also feels given, from some great beyond, an experience so unexpected and profound that one can only try to take it in. At the same time, joy leaves a lasting impression, one that comes to the surface just as grief does, in the most ordinary of days. The experience of joy is not fleeting or shallow, but deep and striking. It is linked to some object of goodness or wonder."[4] Joy is found at the intersection of past and future, memory and present, lament and hope.

My mama died in December of 2013, in the season of Advent. It's a whole season dedicated to waiting, to the knowledge that something promised is not yet come in its fullness, but we are expecting it until it arrives, and we will live into its future. It's a season of prolepsis.

In the Advent of December 2013, we waited for my sister and her family to arrive from Alaska, we waited for the Christ child to come, and we waited for my mother to die. I do not mean an impatient-looking-at-our-watches-can-we-get-on-with-it waiting; I mean wait as in holding vigil.

The progression of her pancreatic cancer had been long and unpleasant at almost every turn. There is nothing buoyant about seeing a loved one collapse, and be collapsed, into the inevitable terminal diagnosis. To make matters worse, we endured an experience with my mother's initial hospital and hospice care that was so bad that when someone asked me, "Do you believe in purgatory now?" I said, "*No!* I now believe in hell!" It was so inexpressibly and inexcusably awful.

And battling the system on top of tending to my mother and our own impending loss, well, we were so weary. So very weary. Yet rather than keeping my mother, whom we love so much, in a situation that was deeply troubling on so many levels, my father and I steeled ourselves to bring her back home.

This approach—namely, tending to her at home—had been our initial preference until the symptoms of her dying became too much for my father and me to manage without an excess of martinis and weeping. We are nothing if not caregivers in our family, and we have no trouble admitting when the need for care has escaped our capacity to offer it.

It had.

But suddenly, thanks to the hospital's ineptitude, we found ourselves again faced with the necessity of bringing her home, and so she came back, and all that Dad and I had going for us was our infinite love for her and for martinis. All other options were closed. And there Dad and I were, faces smashed into finitude in many and various ways.

So I packed up suitcases for my two children and me to move in again with Dad, and with the help of a new hospice organization, we arranged for medical equipment to be delivered to their home, and we reprinted the med charts we had created the first time around, hoping to God that they'd help us from making her troubles any worse by underdosing or overdosing her, and Dad readied the house to take his wife back for the last time.

And then, only hours before we were to bring her home, the blessed hospice called, the Dougherty Hospice House in Sioux Falls, South Dakota (may God forever bless the Dougherty House in Sioux Falls), and the woman at the other end of the phone said, like a clarion call in the night, like an angel over a field of shepherds watching at night, "There *is* room in the inn!"

So we piled Mom into Karl's wheelchair-accessible seat in our van, left the hospital, kept going straight instead of taking a right, and brought my mother to the hospice door, and a volunteer greeted us with no sign of pity but instead radiant hospitality and said, "I know just what room you'll be in." She then looked into my eyes and my soul and, seeing my weariness and grief and anger, continued, "And you look like you need a cookie. I'll bring a plate of them and hot coffee right on down once you get settled."

And I could barely hold it together. "That," I squeaked, "would be very fine."

Up until that point, Dad and I, who each have a habit of coping by using humor that sometimes verges on the inappropriate, had been praying a familiar prayer, but with a twist. Rather than a quiet and pious, "Come, Lord Jesus, be our guest," we offered it more like this: "*Come*, Lord Jesus, *be our guest!*"

You do it.

We are pooped. (That's vernacular for "We are finite.")

No amount of martinis and tears are going to help us this time.

We. Are. Pooped.

Finite.

Finis.

If you're going to come, then come already.

And then we got a call, and cookies, and coffee, and suddenly there was a bit of the infinite breathing into our tired sails. Jesus showed up in the form of a phone call, a welcoming woman, and a cookie.

Advent is the season where the finite yearns for the infinite, and in its infinite mystery, every now and again we catch a glimpse of it. Advent is the season of promises, the season in which we acknowledge that if everything were as it should be, we wouldn't need the promises. But given that we are finite and things aren't all as they are supposed to be (we could just as easily *not* have received that call, and we are fully aware that many people don't), we can at least bend toward the promises, maybe even acting into them and out of them.

Advent is the season of reminders that beginnings lead to endings and endings lead to beginnings. And Advent tells us that this cycle is one of both painful truth and defiant hope and even, in the shape of a cookie, joy.

Advent is the season of becoming incarnate: not just the Son of God as the very Son of Mary but Christians into Christ-made-known. Turns out, Advent gives us a terrific tune about finitude, though I concede it doesn't use the word, and while it doesn't use the word *joy* either, joy threads through all its lyrics. It goes like this:

> *Each winter as the year grows older,*
> *we each grow older too.*

The chill sets in a little colder.
The verities we knew seem shaken and untrue.
When race and class cry out for treason,
when sirens call for war,
they overshout the voice of reason
and scream till we ignore all we held dear before.
Yet I believe beyond believing
that life can spring from death,
that growth can flower from our grieving
that we can catch our breath
and turn transfixed by faith.
So even as the sun is turning
to journey to the north
the living flame in secret burning
can kindle on the earth
and bring God's love to birth.
O child of ecstasy and sorrows,
O Prince of peace and pain,
brighten today's world by tomorrow's
renew our lives again
Lord Jesus come and reign![5]

On the day before my mama died, she was essentially comatose, such that I began to clear out her things: her sweater, the coffeepot, and our secret stash of gin. My mama loved her gin.

I left the Christmas decorations on the wall, on the off chance that her eyes would open and she'd see the holiday delight.

All night I expected The Call.

But by that morning, it still hadn't come.

So I went back to hospice the next morning and found her as I'd left her. Once in her room, I touched her gently and told her that I'd arrived. She smiled faintly, eyes closed. I said I was going to make some coffee and then be right back. Her eyebrows went up, eyes still closed. I asked her if she wanted some of my strong coffee, and she mumbled that she did and nodded.

So I made some press-pot brew, found a swab, rinsed the mint flavor out of it, dabbed it in the cup, and offered it to my mother.

She barely opened her mouth for the swab, but when the coffee hit her lips, her eyes flew open, and she said, "Ooooooohhhhhh, that . . . is . . . so . . . gooooooood." And she asked to sit up, and she had more coffee, and she had a very little lunch and said a little of this and a little of that. Dad and I were stunned, and he joked with her that perhaps now all she needed was a little gin.

This time, her eyes got really big, and she said, "*Yes!*"

Dad started to look for the gin bottle.

I stared at Dad.

Then I looked at my mother, who knew me better than I knew myself, and she was already staring at me.

"Um . . ." I said. "Mom?"

She kept staring at me.

"There's . . . well, there's no way to delicately say this." I took a deep breath and then talked fast. "So . . . I thought that you'd had your last gin last night, so I brought the bottle home and hoisted one to you from my living room. The bottle"—I gulped—"is still there."

Silence.

"Do you want me to go home and get it?"

She grinned. This woman on the edge of death grinned. "Yes, Anna Margrethe. Yes. I. Do."

And I did.

And we hoisted.

And we drank.

And even in that moment of dying, there was life, and there was joy.

———

N. T. Wright has noticed that the texts that involve joy fall into one of two categories: either joy experienced *because* of something or joy experienced *notwithstanding* something. Within these two metagroups, Wright sifts out the biblical texts even further, breaking them down into ones that refer to joy experienced during occasions of celebration and relationships as well as by way of good food and wine, joy that is felt in contrast to sorrow and in thanksgiving for God's redemptive presence and relief, and joy found in the form of peace in the midst of distress.[6]

To the first, he references the joy that is impossible to know without God. Psalm 16, for example, begins with "I say to the Lord, 'You are my Lord; I have no good apart from you'" (16:2) and wraps up with "You show me the path of life. In your presence there is fullness of joy; in your right hand are pleasures forevermore" (16:11). Even nature, Scripture reveals, can experience a joy so deep that it can only be rooted in God, as we hear in the prophet Joel: "Do not fear, O soil; be glad and rejoice, for the Lord has done great things! Do not fear, you animals of the field, for the pastures of the wilderness are green; the tree bears its fruit, the fig tree and vine give their full yield" (2:21–22). In both cases, the joy stems from a certainty that God is the Creator, a gratitude for the Creator God's continuing presence in life, and a trust that God will remain with creature and creation steadfastly, ultimately, and with compassion.

Perhaps one of the most famous texts on joy in this regard comes from Psalm 30:5: "His anger is but for a moment; his favor is for a lifetime. Weeping may linger for the night, but joy comes with the morning."

Isaiah 24:11 is bleak: "There is an outcry in the streets for lack of wine; all joy has reached its eventide; the gladness of the earth is banished." And yet Isaiah 35:1–2 speaks of consolation and, in fact, joy: "The wilderness and the dry land shall be glad, the desert shall rejoice and blossom; like the crocus it shall blossom abundantly, and rejoice with joy and singing."

And in those days, when there is relief from suffering, there is promise that even God will enter into the rejoicing, as in Zephaniah: "On that day it shall be said to Jerusalem: Do not fear, O Zion; do not let your hands grow weak. The Lord, your God, is in your midst, a warrior who gives victory; he will rejoice over you with gladness, he will renew you in his love; he will exult over you with loud singing as on a day of festival" (3:16–18).

Luke 15:4–7, 8–10 tells of the joy of finding a sheep and finding a coin, neither of which did anything *to be* found, other than to be lost. But the finding causes the finder joy. These are scriptural testimonies that joy can be found in the midst of distress thanks to the memory of God having made good on God's promises in the past and the trust that God's persisting promises always throw us into the future of God.

And we can rejoice that we are accompanied by others, that we are part of the Communion of Saints, that joy can and will be made complete in the company of others. Take these passages from Philippians: "I thank my God every time I remember you, constantly praying with joy in every one of my prayers for all of you, because of your sharing in the gospel from the first day until now" (1:3–5), or "What does it matter? Just this, that Christ is proclaimed in every way, whether out of false motives or true; and in that I rejoice" (1:18), or "If then there is any encouragement in Christ, any consolation from love, any sharing in the Spirit, any compassion and sympathy, make my joy complete: be of the same mind, having the same love, being in full accord and of one mind" (2:1–2), or "Rejoice in the Lord always; again I will say, Rejoice" (4:4).

And Jesus's words to his disciples in the Gospel of John: "As the Father has loved me, so I have loved you; abide in my love. If you keep my commandments, you will abide in my love, just as I have kept my Father's commandments and abide in his love. I have said these things to you so that my joy may be in you, and that your joy may be complete" (15:9–11).

Each of these texts knows of the consolation of camaraderie, of the presence and prayers of other supporters, and of the fidelity of God both in the midst of the suffering and with eschatological promise proleptically plowed into the present.

———

I do believe that two years into the Covid pandemic, the word *limit* should enter the adult language lexicon. Those so-last-year normal, garden-variety limits we faced regularly—like the limits of time, budget, abilities, vocational options, caloric intake, viable dreams—these limits were already tiresome.

But nowadays, thanks to the pandemic, we face all of those *and* we have to extend our list to include limited gatherings, limited worship, limited school days, limited work, limited eating out, limited travel, limited recreation, limited finances, limited patience, and limited time.

It turns out that *limit* comes from the Latin word *limitem*, meaning "a boundary or a border."

And *limitem* also forms the basis for the word *liminal*, or "a place at the threshold." A liminal space, then, is the in-between space between limits. It's a disorienting, mysterious, nebulous, scary, and thrilling place all at once, and in its midst, a person is helpless, faced by an infinite set of options compressed, paradoxically, within a very finite set of limits.

It's a bit like Holy Saturday.

It's a bit like life.

———

Liturgical Christians inaugurate the season of Lent with Ash Wednesday, and a defining mark, so to speak, of the service is the imprint of a definitive limit on our foreheads.

On that day, every time we look at ourselves in the mirror or when we look at others—who are mirrors themselves of our own mortality—we are reminded of the most inhibiting limit of all: that of death.

From the inception of the season (Ash Wednesday) to its culmination (Good Friday), Lent is both framed by and imbued with the notion of limits. The whole point of the season is that limits don't just happen; we are, essentially—that is, in our very essence—limited. So it shouldn't be any surprise that the Christian tradition has taken this season straight on down the path of solemnity.

Lent is a reminder of that which we already know but try—and we really are quite masterful in our attempts—to escape.

We are limited.

We are born; we die.

"You are dust, and to dust you shall return" (Gen 3:19).

Talk about limits.

That's a pretty clear set of brackets we've got there. And everything—even our capacity for good, say Christians—is limited by them. The only thing that isn't limited is our need for redemption. And perhaps imagination. That and, thankfully, God's grace.

Nonetheless, I get it. I do. I understand why we have, as a tradition, dedicated the intentional time of Lent to the deep value of focusing on our mortality, our sinfulness, our need for repentance.

But this past year, I entered the season of Lent differently because I was and am in a liminal space of loving someone. So apropos to liminality, everything is informed by that utterly disorienting, mysterious, nebulous, scary, and thrilling truth, and I am helpless in its midst.

It turns out that among David's many virtues, he happens to have fine taste in music.

He's introduced me to all sorts of tunes by different artists in a variety of genres and with distinct lyrical themes. My repertoire is about caught up to where it should have been long ago.

I am now way, way hipper than I was, and were that not such a low bar to cross, it would be a substantially more impressive announcement than it appears to be.

Of all of the music he's sent my way, the lyrics of one song in particular have grabbed my attention: Jason Isbell's "If We Were Vampires." It's a love song, to be sure, but not your garden-variety love song—as the title itself makes clear. You hear "vampire," and you think "I want to suck your blood," which is not in the top ten list of successful come-on lines, let's be frank.

But the point of Isbell's tune is not about capes and long teeth but rather about limits—or, rather, the lack of them.

When you aren't bounded by the limit of mortality, Isbell's lyrics sing, the value of everything is diminished. In fact, the value of everything is empty, is lost. In a video interview, Isbell explains what moved him to write this song.[7] He says he began to ask himself these questions: "What is it, really? Really? Why do I care? Why does anybody care about anybody else to make themselves this vulnerable?"

And then it dawns on him: "This is it. That's all we get. We get this time on earth and then that's it. We don't know what's next, if anything." It's true, he says, that his beloved's dress is beautiful, and so is she. Her trust in him, her love for him, her support of him, these are also all true. But Isbell sings this truer truth: neither her dress, nor her beauty, nor her vulnerability, nor her love for him, nor even their lovemaking, none of these would matter, none of it at all, if the truth of it all weren't fleeting.

Exhale.

My love and I both know the truth of the death of one whom we've cherished.

The risk of falling in love again, the risk of embracing another, the risk of loss—it's all inexpressibly risky. And yet here we are, drawn to this liminal space.

But why is any of this risky?

Because love is, life is, temporal.

Everything can, and will, end.

And that, right there, that is why love is, life is, beautiful. None of it can be taken for granted because it could be gone in an instant. Precisely because of that, then, love and life are to be treasured, delighted in, cherished, and protected. We are to stand in wondrous awe of it all.

Some time back, my father told me of a Jewish tale he's heard along the way. He can't quite place it, he said, but the gist of it is that a man died, met his maker, and found God staring at him sternly. "Why," asked God of the man, "why did you not delight in the gift of my creation while you were alive?"

I would love to find the story, but even as it stands in its incompleteness, it offers holy truth.

Lent, like life, is liminal. Distinct from the normal pattern of life, in Lent, we begin with death and end with new life. We have forty days within to focus on anything, anything at all.

It is worth noting that the opposite of death is not life but birth. Life, *life* is what happens in between those markers. So Lent actually is a season of life!

Instead, what do we do with it? We tend to turn the focus of these forty days onto death.

What, I wonder, would happen if we turned our Lenten focus instead on finite life?

What would happen if we began to consider Lent from the perspective of liminality, like Isbell invites lovers to do? I can't help but wonder what would happen if we would instead engage the season less with somberness and more with gratitude not driven by guilt but rather infused by delight and illuminated by joy. I wonder if we would see Lent as a time that invites us to savor life as long as we can; to steward ourselves as well as possible; to sit in perplexed, astonished wonderment of it all; even (gasp! in Lent!) to celebrate the goodness that is God's gift of creation all year long.

Life is fleeting.

Life is limited.

Therefore, life is all the more to be embraced—and, paradoxically, embraced with no limits at all to our love of it, our joy in it.

———

Every year I say it, and so I will say it again this year: Holy Saturday is the most honest day of the church. It is the vortex of pain and balm, grief and comfort, rage and reconciliation, despair and hope. We have a foot in each truth on this day: things as they are and things as they will be. Here's a distinct difference, though, between this Holy Saturday and the first one: in contrast to those living at the time of Jesus's dying, we know it's Holy Saturday.

To those who loved Jesus—and, for that matter, those who hated him or were indifferent to him—it was . . . Saturday. For Jesus's own people, Saturday was the Sabbath. I do not mean to diminish the sacredness of that weekly, holy observance, but it was a Saturday, it was a Sabbath, like any other, excepting the rocking, wrecking, wrenching grief of Jesus's crucifixion the day before.

The women didn't know what they would find—or wouldn't find—come the next morning.

And the men didn't even come to look. Nobody knew anything about angels or gardeners or the fear they would experience when faced with the resurrection news. All they knew was despondency. But we do know something about angels and gardeners and fear because we know the story. We know that Jesus got himself on up, declared himself hungry (well deserved, to be sure), and announced that death doesn't win.

But the Holy Saturdays in our lives can mess us up precisely because we know the story.

We know by faith that resurrection happens, and if it did then, why not now? When someone we love is gravely injured and ill, we cling to the hope that resurrection will happen, because it did way back on that day. When we have lived through troubled times with a loved one who sabotages trust and spirits and even Self, we keep staying Saturday after Saturday after Saturday, on the edge of our seat for that sure-to-be-coming Sunday that never seems to come on our calendar.

Think about addictions or harmful habits or personal/relational/vocational patterns we have known all too well. We also know too well the hope that this time . . . this time . . . we have given them up, we have broken them down, we have stopped them in their tracks . . . and then Friday comes again, but never Sunday.

I've written earlier about the line I heard a while back: the amount of pain in your life is commensurate with the distance between your reality and your expectations. Back on that first Holy Saturday, those surrounding Jesus knew only the reality of his death and had no expectation of his renewed life. We, in contrast, know the reality of his death (and any number of variations on that theme in our own lives), *and* we know to expect not just his resurrection but ours.

And that resurrection changes our perception of reality and expectations. It frees us to reevaluate our reality and our expectations. We are liberated to consider changing not just our expectations (typically by first considering lowering them) but our very reality.

For those of us who know about Holy Sunday, Holy Saturday is where the stirring to reconsider everything begins. We can hope for complete healing, or we can trust that death doesn't win and we refuse to cede to it our spirits too. We can hope for relational reconciliation, or we can see that the resurrection will come not from within a toxic person or dynamic but by leaving that person or dynamic behind.

We can hope to break out of harmful self-sabotage, or we can see our return to wellness as incremental, as a work in progress, as a reminder that we are still here, with breath to change, to fight, to become whole again, to live—and die—another day, to sample foretastes, maybe even a full hearty glass, of joy.

Holy Saturday doesn't eliminate pain.

It reframes it.

The story of my late husband's German memorial service, mentioned in the introduction, has even more layers to the moment. "A Mighty Fortress Is Our God" was Bill's favorite hymn; singing it at his funeral was obvious to me. But while we sung this Lutheran anthem, so dear to his heart, sweet tiny Karl was in the ICU, and the docs were waiting for our return from the worship to begin to wean Karl out of the induced coma. There were no guarantees about whether my boy would rise up and out of the coma even so. With this emotional fusion as the backdrop, we got to this verse:

God's Word forever shall abide
no thanks to foes, who fear it.
For God himself fights by our side
with weapons of the Spirit.
Were they to take our house,
goods, honor, child, or spouse,
though life be wrenched away,
they cannot win the day,
The kingdom's ours forever![8]

I leaned over to my father, who was sitting right next to me, and I said, "Death thinks it's won. It's just pissed me off." And it has: anger is a form of defiance, of recognizing the unrighteousness of something and then making use of that brain-driven, hormone-fueled, principle-grounded compulsion to fight back.

But joy is another way to reject death's power, to refute it, and at least for the moment, to be more powerful than it.

Like straw into gold, despair is spun into defiance, and anger is spun into joy.

———

Several months after Bill's German memorial service, we were back at Trinity Lutheran Seminary, where he and I had met, for his memorial service. Bill had been cremated in Germany and his remains brought back by a friend of the family to stay in their sunroom until we could pick up the urn upon our return to the States. Bill spent two months overlooking South Dakota prairie and then ten months in the workroom that he'd looked so forward to having. And after this Ohio service, he would be buried in a plot on the South Dakota prairie in the same cemetery as my grandparents, and where my mama now is buried, and where my father and I will one day too. We'd brought his urn along with us to Columbus for the service as a tangible reminder to all of Bill.

When we arrived at the seminary, I was exhausted. Emotionally, physically pooped. So I took a nap. I set my phone alarm for an hour before the service, thinking that was just enough time to ready myself and my kidlets before walking across to the chapel to greet not just guests but the real Communion of the Saints who had breathed and believed for us in the darkest moments of our little world.

Thirty minutes later, my dearest friend burst into the room. "Anna!" Sarah cried. "The service starts in a half an hour!" I shot up, looked at my phone, and breathed relief that she was so very wrong. "Woman," I replied, "let me sleep. Look. I have another hour." And I showed her my phone so she could see the time. Sarah looked at it, looked at me, and silently pointed to the clock in the room. And in a very steady, firm, and yet somehow loving voice, she said, "Anna, dear one. Your phone hasn't switched time zones. You have thirty minutes. You need to Get. Up. Now." Naturally, it was about this time that our beloved caregiver, Jason (we dubbed him our "manny"), also staying in the apartment, realized that he'd forgotten to bring his dress shoes.

So I sprung out of bed and phoned friend and mentor in many things, not least of all martinis and manhattans, Walter Bouman to see what his shoe size was. It was a half size off, but it would do. Jason and Karl dashed to pick up the shoes while I threw on my dress and threw out Else's diapers and wanted very much to throw up.

With ten minutes to spare, eighteen-month-old Else and I raced our way to her papa's memorial service, where had we not met, this little girl wouldn't even be in my arms at all, nor would this tragedy have taken place.

And then, all of a sudden, Else—this girl who was and is so profound and wise but at that age and at that moment had no idea of the magnitude of the event at hand—right then, this tiny thing bouncing along on my hip stuck out her finger, held it high like a lantern, and began to sing in her tiny but clarion voice, "This little light of mine, I'm going to let it shine." I looked at her, my eyes and mouth wide open—her, of all people, at this very dark moment, singing the gospel to me. And so what could I do? I put out my finger just like she had, tears flowing, and I began to sing with her: "This little light of mine, I'm gonna let it shine." It was that moment, right between line two and three of this children's song, this revolutionary song, this gospel song, when it dawned on me:

"Wait a minute. Wait one little minute. Elsegirl is in *this* hand. The light of Jesus is in *this* hand. *Where is Bill?*"

And then I realized that he was still on the coffee table back at seminary housing. Not only did I almost miss Bill's memorial service. So did he.

Sometimes, let's be honest, the Christ light might for all the world seem to be snuffed out, as when mourning death or divorce or experiencing chronic disease or addiction or depression or suffering or injustice or painful conflict or doubt.

That's Good Friday. Bleak. Inky.

Sometimes, however, the light may be overwhelmingly bright. It might be at the birth of a child. It might be when love breaks in. It might be at an exquisite feast or concert or when an event was pulled off with fewer snags and more sense of the Spirit than possibly imaginable. It might be when a call is affirmed. It might be when the Minnesota Twins win the World Series.

And sometimes, the Christ light might be glowing sure enough but might be somewhat hidden, dimmed, like during periods of exhaustion, or confusion, or distraction, or loneliness, or conflict. Perhaps we've simply moved away from the light, apathy or another shiny something catching our attention, leading us to a light that may illuminate but is illusory.

On Holy Saturday, the light shines, but not in its fullness. Darkness still has a real presence; it still tempers the light . . . and yet. And yet we lean toward, yearn for, the light. We begin to see its glow, even if faint, as in the Easter Vigil, because bleakness will not overcome it, even if it feels like it has a real fighting chance to do just that.

––––––––––

June 18, 2004, taught me as much about joy as everything that has occurred since.

On that day, all was mostly well in my world. Worst complaint was that I was away from my son, just shy of three years old, when he burned his finger on a stove. Little eight-month-old Else and I were gone, honoring my doctoral advisor at a fest in a small town some ways away.

Bill and Karl had stayed back in Regensburg, packing and planning for the next month's big move back to the United States after five near-perfect years in Germany.

"I'll kiss it when I see you on Sunday, sweet boy!" I said. "OK, Mama!" Karl said. "Ich vermisse dich!" he said. I miss you!

The next time I saw Karl, I had just left the corpse of his father in the neighboring hospital's morgue, and my sweet, sweet Karlchen was wrapped in blankets, attached to tubes, his tiny finger swaddled in a white bandage, his tiny head swaddled in a turban of white bandages dotted with iodine and blood.

Baby Else was being passed around, cooing and wooing the ICU staff in the bowels of the hospital that would be our home for the next six long weeks.

In some ways, June 18 is far worse than June 19, the day when All Things Changed.

We were oblivious on June 18—positively oblivious—not only to what *would* happen the next day but that it even *could*. Every year since, I brace myself for June 18, for it is a day filled with taunts of "what-if."

What if I had insisted that Karl and Bill come along to this retreat?

What if they had missed the bus instead of catching it?

What if they'd been ahead of schedule . . . whatever their schedule was that day?

What if they had hadn't decided to go to . . . wherever it was that they were heading?

What if Bill had instead said, "Ah, the heck with it. Let's go get an ice cream, Karlchen!"

What if, what if, whatif whatifwhatifwhatifwhatifwhatif whatif . . .

It's a question that can become a repetitive sound, as annoying as a leaky faucet drip that can't be fixed, as a snore that can't be turned over, as an earworm that you can't get out of your head no matter how many countermelodies you try to hum. But it also is a question that, as a German might say, "Bringt aber nichts."

It doesn't bring anything.

It doesn't bring a damn thing . . . except unresolved, and unresolvable, possibilities.

These possibilities are the "may-haves."

They may have not been hit by the car at all.

They may have surprised me in Neuentdettelsau.

They may even have gotten all the packing for our move done! Wouldn't *that* have been fantastic!

Karl may have gone on to be a hiker and a linguist and a world traveler.

Bill may have found his dream vocational fit back home.

But of course, one day, it dawned on me that the "may-haves" can take a person anywhere.

Instead of being the designer of world peace (as I naturally had envisioned him to be), Karl may have been called up in some unforeseen terrible war and both inflicted and suffered great trauma.

Instead of being the victim of an accident, Bill may have been the perpetrator of one that caused even more death and grief.

Any number of other difficulties may have befallen us: addiction, depression, betrayal, anger, disease, who knows?

One day it clicked that we may have been equally broken, just in a different, unknown way.

Who really knows?

In the end, what-ifs, may-haves—a pox on both.

A pox on both.

All I know for sure is that what I had on June 18, 2004, was beautiful. And what I had on June 19 was not. And that much of what came after June 19 was not. But I also know that every breakthrough that Karl has made after that awful accident I have held, I have treasured, I have claimed, I have known that, at least for the moment, was Karl's, it was Else's, it was mine.

Even the 19th couldn't take away Karl learning to say "E" again and unfolding his left hand again and—oh, Good God have mercy—Karl smiling again.

Even the 19th couldn't take away the way that Else and Karl protest that day with their laughter, and their love, and their strong spirits, and their regular forgiveness of their worn-out, stressed-out, tapped-out mama, and their trust that they are deeply, deeply loved.

Even the 19th couldn't take away the Communion of the Saints, those who breathed and believed on days when I could not.

Although no one can prove *that* he said it, people like to *say* that Martin Luther once proclaimed that if he found that the world would end tomorrow, he would plant an apple tree today. I've asked myself, if I'd known on the 18th that Bill and Karl would have been mercilessly and unalterably hit by that car on the 19th, what would I have done? Well, I would have clearly left that conference to kiss that thumb, that much I know.

But would I have spent my last moments with them clinging to them? Would I have sent my fingernails into them, gripping them away from what was to come? Would I have wiped my tears on them, spent my last hours wailing?

Honestly?

Probably.

But I like to think that I wouldn't have anyway. And I like to live now like I wouldn't anyway. Not only did the 19th teach me that some things can't be taken away; it has taught me that some things have been given to me, indelibly pressed into me, things that also cannot be taken away.

Like this: the accident taught me that I don't know what tomorrow will bring. It *could* bring death and despair. Or it could bring deep gladness and joy. Or . . . it could be really dull. Ordinary. Utterly noneventful. I simply don't know.

I *do* know, however, what I want *this* day to be, *this* moment to be a day, a moment of rich love and kindness and gratitude and joy.

Not only can the 19th not take that away from me, but the 19th has *given* it to me, this new appreciation that we have one another, that every moment is sacred, that *we* are sacred, and that, as I tell the kids, our love and kindness and joy can be contagious to others, perhaps even making the world just a little more loving, more kind, and more joyful.

My children, these two tangible Easters of mine who live in our steady stream of Holy Saturdays, I simply *refuse* to have them grow up in a world where they have seen their mother fretful all the time.

That isn't to say that I'm *not* fretful all the time (good Lord do I worry), but Karl and Else remind me to shed my fear—or at least to tamp it down—to trust not the fickle (but powerfully tempting) what-ifs and may-haves. Instead, they remind me that there is life to live here.

There is gratitude to embrace.

There is joy to be had.

There is a moment, a present moment, that is a gift to be shared not only with one another but also with the future, whatever it may be.

I confess that I can't think about the 18th and how perfect it was, and I still can't look at pictures from before the accident, and I have videos from those days that I doubt I'll ever see again.

It's too painful. And I admit that I can't think back to and linger on that terrible 19th.

But I can write, with full integrity and honesty, that I can now, almost two decades hence, declare that every moment is sacred, every moment is to be savored, every moment is a possibility to plant a tree, to plant a promise, to plant joyful defiance.

The Eve of Grief is also an Eve of *Doch*.

Death is real. And it is terrible. It hurts, and it says and it seems for all the world that it has the last word. That it has won.

But life, on this eve of whatever tomorrow will bring, is real-er.

Doch, Doch, Doch.

Notes

Chapter 1

1 Lester Meyer, "A Lack of Laments in the Church's Use of the Psalter," *Lutheran Quarterly* 7 (Spring 1993): 67–78.

2 Meyer, 67–68.

3 Meyer, 69.

4 *Lutheran Book of Worship: Ministers Desk Edition* (Minneapolis: Augsburg, 1978), 340–440.

5 Meyer, "Lack of Laments," 72.

6 Meyer, 72.

7 Meyer, 72; and Robert Davidson, *The Courage to Doubt: Exploring an Old Testament Theme* (London: SCM, 1983), 91–92, drawing here also on the work of Samuel E. Balentine, *The Hidden God: The Hiding of the Face of God in the Old Testament* (Oxford: Oxford University Press, 1983), 171–72.

8 Meyer, "Lack of Laments," 76, referring to Walter Brueggemann, *The Message of the Psalms: A Theological Commentary* (Minneapolis: Augsburg, 1984), 11, 53.

9 Walter Brueggemann, *Israel's Praise: Doxology against Idolatry and Ideology* (Philadelphia: Fortress, 1988), 137.

10 For more on this point, see my book *I Can Do No Other: The Church's New Here We Stand Moment* (Minneapolis: Fortress, 2019).

11 Tom Christenson, "A Place for Honest Questioning," Concordia College Alumni News, Spring 1980, 37.

12 Christenson.

13 Cornel West, "Subversive Joy and Revolutionary Patience in Black Christianity," in *The Cornel West Reader* (New York: Basic Civitas, Perseus, 1999), 437.

14 Martin Luther, "Heidelberg Disputation (1518)," in *Martin Luther's Basic Theological Writings*, ed. Timothy Lull (Minneapolis: Fortress, 1989), 49.

15 Walter Brueggemann, *Deep Memory, Exuberant Hope: Contested Truth in a Post-Christian World*, ed. Patrick D. Miller (Minneapolis: Fortress, 2000), 62.

16 Soraya Chemaly, *Rage Becomes Her: The Power of Women's Anger* (New York: Atria, 2018).

17 Chemaly, 251.

18 Chemaly, xx.

19 Chemaly, xiii.

20 Brueggemann, *Deep Memory*, 61.

21 Brueggemann, 61.

22 Gordon Lathrop, "What Are We Hoping For?," *Accent on Worship* 3/4 (1985).

23 Barbara Ehrenreich, *Bright-Sided: How the Relentless Promotion of Positive Thinking Has Undermined America* (New York: Metropolitan Books, 2009), 43–44.

24 Annie Dillard, *Holy the Firm* (New York: Harper & Row, 1977), 58–59.

25 Brueggemann, *Deep Memory*, 60.

26 Dominique D. Gilliard, "Dominique D. Gilliard: Reclaiming the Power of Lament," Faith and Leadership, August 25, 2015, https://faithandleadership.com/dominique-d-gilliard-reclaiming-power-lament.

27 Gilliard.

28 Elie Wiesel, "Hope, Despair and Memory," lecture, Nobel Prize, December 11, 1986, https://www.nobelprize.org/prizes/peace/1986/wiesel/lecture/.

29 Rev. Dr. William Flippin, "Grounded in Grace: You Visited Me," *Living Lutheran*, July 25, 2016, 5, https://www.livinglutheran .org/2016/07/grounded-in-grace/.

30 Martin Luther King Jr., "Loving Your Enemies," in *Strength to Love* (1963; repr., Philadelphia: Fortress, 1981), 53.

31 Brueggemann, *Deep Memory*, 106.

32 Walter Brueggemann, *Mandate to Difference: An Invitation to the Contemporary Church* (Louisville: Westminster John Knox, 2007), 131.

33 Gilliard, "Reclaiming."

34 Madsen, *I Can Do No Other*.

35 West, "Subversive Joy," 437.

36 See Brueggemann, *Deep Memory*, 60–61.

37 Elie Wiesel, "Ich habe einen Traum," *Die Zeit* 5 (January 27, 2000): 16.

Chapter 2

1 Brueggemann, *Israel's Praise*, 92–93.

2 Luther, "Heidelberg Disputation (1518)," 49.

3 More details can be found in Madsen, *I Can Do No Other*.

4 Brueggemann, *Israel's Praise*, 136.

5 Brueggemann, 146.

6 Brueggemann, 147–48.

7 Brueggemann, 148.

8 Ehrenreich, *Bright-Sided*, 32.

9 Ehrenreich, 12–13.

10 Mihaly Csikszentmihalyi, *Flow: The Psychology of Optimal Experience* (New York: HarperPerennial, 1990), 44.

11 Csikszentmihalyi, 44.

12 Jürgen Moltmann, "Christianity: A Religion of Joy," in *Joy and Human Flourishing: Essays on Theology, Culture, and the Good*

Life, ed. Miroslav Volf and Justin E. Crisp (Minneapolis: Fortress, 2015), 11.

13 Moltmann, 11.

14 Friedrich Schiller, "An die Freude / Ode to Joy," Schiller Institute, https://archive.schillerinstitute.com/transl/schiller_poem/ode_to_joy.pdf.

15 Moltmann, "Christianity," 12–14.

16 Moltmann, 15.

17 Miroslav Volf, "The Crown of the Good Life: A Hypothesis," in Volf and Crisp, *Joy and Human Flourishing*, 127.

18 Marianne Meye Thompson, "Reflections on Joy in the Bible," in Volf and Crisp, *Joy and Human Flourishing*, 33.

19 Paul Gruchow, *The Necessity of Empty Places* (New York: St. Martin's, 1988), 135.

20 Terms associated with family systems theory. See Craig L. Nessan, "Surviving Congregational Leadership: A Theology of Family Systems," *Word & World* 20, no. 4 (Fall 2000).

21 Csikszentmihalyi, *Flow*, 54.

22 Patrick Kelly, "Experiencing Life's Flow: Sports and the Spiritual Life," *America: The Jesuit Review* 199, no. 12 (October 20, 2008).

23 Frederick Buechner, *Wishful Thinking: A Theological ABC* (New York: Harper & Row, 1973), 95.

24 Paul Tillich, *Love, Power, and Justice* (1954; repr., London: Oxford, 1974), 30.

25 Tillich, 31.

26 Paul Tillich, *The New Being* (New York: Scribner's, 1955), 145, 146.

27 Alexander Irwin, *Eros toward the World: Paul Tillich and the Theology of the Erotic* (Minneapolis: Fortress, 1991). See particularly his chapter "Tillich's Eros and Feminist/Womanist Theologies: Toward the Theological Future," 153–96.

28 Irwin, 87.

29 N. T. Wright, "Joy: Some New Testament Perspectives and Questions," in Volf and Crisp, *Joy and Human Flourishing*, 42.

30 Allan Aubrey Boesak, *Searching for a Language of Life in Faith and Politics* (Grand Rapids, MI: Eerdmans, 2014), 2.

Chapter 3

1 National Alliance on Mental Illness, "Mental Health by the Numbers," last updated March 2021, https://nami.org/mhstats.

2 Alice Park, "How the Tokyo Olympics Changed the Conversation about Athletes' Mental Health," *Time*, August 8, 2021, https://time.com/6088078/mental-health-olympics-simone-biles/.

3 Dalai Lama and Desmond Tutu with Douglas Abrams, *The Book of Joy: Lasting Happiness in a Changing World* (New York: Penguin, 2016), 110.

4 Chemaly, *Rage Becomes Her*, 37.

5 Dalai Lama, Tutu, and Abrams, *Book of Joy*, 110; see also Park, "How the Tokyo Olympics Changed."

6 Chemaly, *Rage Becomes Her*, 295.

7 Esther Sternberg, "The Science of Healing Places," *On Being with Krista Tippett*, originally aired on September 27, 2012, updated on October 24, 2013, https://onbeing.org/programs/esther-sternberg-the-science-of-healing-places/#transcript.

8 Darby Kathleen Ray, "It's about Time: Reflections on a Theology of Rest," in *Theology That Matters: Ecology, Economy, and God*, ed. Darby Kathleen Ray (Minneapolis: Fortress, 2006), 159–60, 161.

9 Suzanne Simard, "Forests Are Wired for Wisdom," *On Being with Krista Tippett*, originally aired on September 9, 2021, https://onbeing.org/programs/suzanne-simard-forests-are-wired-for-wisdom/.

10 Simard. You can find Simard's work at the Mother Tree Project: https://www.mothertreeproject.org.

11 Michael Unger, "Put Down the Self-Help Books: Resilience Is Not a DIY Endeavor," *Globe and Mail*, May 25, 2019.

12 Andrea Mazzarino, "How to Cope with Government-Induced Stress," *Nation*, February 7, 2020, https://www.thenation.com/article/world/government-induced-stress/.

13 Resmaa Menakem, *My Grandmother's Hands: Racialized Trauma and the Pathway to Mending Our Hearts and Bodies* (Las Vegas: Central Recovery, 2017), 138.

14 Menakem, 169.

15 From Brené Brown, "The Courage to Be Vulnerable," *On Being with Krista Tippett*, originally aired on November 22, 2012, updated January 29, 2015, https://onbeing.org/programs/brene-brown-the-courage-to-be-vulnerable-jan2015/.

16 Brown.

17 Menakem, *My Grandmother's Hands*, 153.

18 Rabbi Danya Ruttenberg, "Go to Yourself," Life Is a Sacred Text, August 23, 2021, https://lifeisasacredtext.substack.com/p/go-to-yourself.

19 Rabbi Danya Ruttenberg, "Why Didn't Abraham Protest on Behalf of His Children?," Life Is a Sacred Text, August 23, 2021, https://lifeisasacredtext.substack.com/p/why-didnt-abraham-protest-on-behalf.

20 Menakem, *My Grandmother's Hands*, 178.

21 Menakem, 19–20.

22 Menakem, 6.

23 Sharon Salzberg, "The Healing Is in the Return," *On Being with Krista Tippett*, originally aired on October 22, 2020, updated August 5, 2021, https://onbeing.org/programs/sharon-salzberg-the-healing-is-in-the-return/.

24 Salzberg.

25 Sternberg, "Science of Healing Places."

26 Adam Grant, "There's a Name for the Blah You're Feeling: It's Called Languishing," *New York Times*, April 19, 2021, updated October 4, 2021. https://t.co/2Kcv4b5NjA.

27 Grant.

28 Teresa M. Amabile and Steven J. Kramer, "The Power of Small Wins," *Harvard Business Review*, May 2011, https://hbr.org/2011/05/the-power-of-small-wins.

29 Dalai Lama, Tutu, and Abrams, *Book of Joy*, 87.

30 Dalai Lama, Tutu, and Abrams, 225.

31 Csikszentmihalyi, *Flow*, 1.

32 Csikszentmihalyi, 92.

33 Gruchow, *Necessity of Empty Places*, 135–37.

Chapter 4

1 Martin Luther, *Luther's Works*, ed. Jaroslav Pelikan (St. Louis, MO: Concordia, 1961), 3:128.

2 Douglas John Hall, *Lighten Our Darkness: Toward an Indigenous Theology of the Cross* (Philadelphia: Westminster, 1976), 214.

3 Anathea Portier-Young, "Commentary on Exodus 3:1–15," Working Preacher, August 31, 2014, https://www.workingpreacher.org/commentaries/revised-common-lectionary/ordinary-22/commentary-on-exodus-31-15-5.

4 "Historical Commentary on the Gospel of Mark, Chapter 12," Historical Commentary on the Gospel of Mark, http://www.michaelturton.com/Mark/GMark12.html#12.p.28.34.

5 "True Self-Love and True Self-Sacrifice," University of Hertfordshire Research Archive, https://uhra.herts.ac.uk/bitstream/handle/2299/9868/903152.pdf;sequence=1. Though the author is unclear, the feminist framework for self-love and self-care is quite helpful.

6 Brown, "Courage to Be Vulnerable."
7 Cornel West, "Christian Love and Heterosexism," in *Cornel West Reader*, 409–10.
8 Cornel West, "A World of Ideas," in *Cornel West Reader*, 299.
9 Toni Morrison, *Beloved* (New York: Vintage International, 2004), 102–4.
10 Dalai Lama, Tutu, and Abrams, *Book of Joy*, 63.

Chapter 5

1 As quoted in Miroslav Volf, *Free of Charge: Giving and Forgiving in a Culture Stripped of Grace* (Grand Rapids, MI: Zondervan, 2009), 127.
2 James H. Cone, *The Cross and the Lynching Tree* (Maryknoll, NY: Orbis, 2011), 18.
3 C. S. Lewis, *Surprised by Joy: The Shape of My Early Life* (New York: Harcourt, 1961), 78.
4 Mary Clark Moschella, "Calling and Compassion: Elements of Joy in Lived Practices of Care," in Volf and Crisp, *Joy and Human Flourishing*, 99.
5 Text by William Gay, Hymn #252, *Evangelical Lutheran Worship* (Minneapolis: Augsburg Fortress, 2006). Copyright © 1971 United Church Press. Reprinted by permission.
6 Wright, "Joy," 39–62.
7 See Isbell perform the song at https://www.youtube.com/watch?v=_d8j8nfTEIk.
8 Martin Luther, Hymn #504, "A Mighty Fortress Is Our God," in *Lutheran Book of Worship*.